NZ Rugby Kitchen

NZ Rugby
Kitchen

CELEBRATING THE LOVE OF FOOD, FAMILY AND RUGBY

RANDOM HOUSE
NEW ZEALAND

NZ
RUGBY FOUNDATION

ALL ROYALTIES TO THE NEW ZEALAND RUGBY FOUNDATION

Photography credits

Kieran Scott: All recipe photography; p2 top, middle left, bottom centre & right; p4; p5 top & centre; p8 top, bottom left; p11 top right, bottom left & right; p12; p16; pp18–19; p22; pp24–25; p36; p44; pp46–47; p48; p78; pp86–87; pp108–109; p116; pp118–119; p136; p142; p144; p146; p150; p158; p168 top right, bottom left; p174 middle left, bottom left, right; p175 middle left & centre, bottom right.

Melanie Jenkins: p2 centre, middle right, bottom left; p5 bottom; p6; p8 bottom right; p10; p11 top left; p30; p60; p62; pp64–65; p68; pp72–73; p76; p80; pp82–83; p94; pp96–97; p104; p112; p126; p130; pp132–133; p151; p168 top left, bottom centre & right; p169; p174 top, centre; p175 top, bottom left; p176.

A RANDOM HOUSE BOOK published by Random House New Zealand
18 Poland Road, Glenfield, Auckland, New Zealand

For more information about our titles go to www.randomhouse.co.nz

A catalogue record for this book is available from the National Library of New Zealand

Random House New Zealand is part of the Random House Group
New York   London   Sydney   Auckland   Delhi   Johannesburg

First published 2012. Reprinted 2012

© 2012 text, New Zealand Rugby Foundation;
photography as credited above

The moral rights of the author have been asserted

ISBN 978 1 77553 003 9

Recipe testing & preparation: Kathy Paterson
Styling: Tamara West
Design: Kate Barraclough
Front cover photograph: Kieran Scott
Back cover photographs: Kieran Scott, left and bottom; Melanie Jenkins, top right. Front and back flap photographs Kieran Scott.

Printed in New Zealand by Printlink

Foreword

MAURICE TRAPP

This is the New Zealand Rugby Foundation's first foray into publishing — we would like to acknowledge the enthusiasm of Random House New Zealand in approaching us to do so.

Given that this year we celebrate our twenty-fifth anniversary it does seem appropriate to venture into new territory to coincide with this important milestone.

It's a great privilege, on behalf of the Board and the many injured players we have supported, to say thank you to Kel Tremain and his family for having the foresight and the passion to create the Foundation twenty-five years ago. Thanks also to Sir Russell Pettigrew for all his work and energy, and for taking on the role of founding president and chairman, and guiding the Foundation from its genesis and through its first ten years.

The original Board of Trustees set down the constitution at a time when rugby was a totally amateur sport and the financial state of many unions was uncertain. These gentlemen had the vision to plan for and then build an organisation that could support rugby over many years. They also had the ability to 'walk the talk', attracting some major beneficiaries and laying down the significant capital that helps sustain our charity today.

Things have moved on significantly since then and our core business now focuses purely on supporting catastrophically injured rugby players financially and emotionally, raising the funds to enable us to support the work we do, partnering with the New Zealand Rugby Union (NZRU) to communicate the message of safety first. The excellent Rugby Smart Programme is a leader in world rugby.

We receive great support every year from a number of organisations. The NZRU provides us with an annual grant that goes directly to fund the needs of our injured players. The New Zealand Rugby Players Association (NZRPA) is also hugely supportive of our work and through this organisation we are able to develop the important link between the professional players and the amateur game where injuries often occur. We also rely heavily on funds we are able to obtain from gaming trusts and our various outstanding sponsors.

Your support by purchasing this book will make a significant collective contribution to our bottom line — thank you! This enables us to be sure that we are there for our players every step of the way.

« **Tane Norton and David Latta, board members of the New Zealand Rugby Foundation.**

Maurice Trapp is the Chairman of the New Zealand Rugby Foundation and Trustee of the New Zealand Spinal Trust. He was Auckland Coach 1987–91. With 93 wins and only 3 losses, they defended and retained the Ranfurly shield for that full period, setting numerous records along the way.

Tane Norton was an All Blacks hooker (1971–77) and captain (1976–77). He played for Canterbury (1969–77) and New Zealand Maori (1969–75 and 1977) and was President of the NZRU (2002–04).

David Latta was an Otago hooker (1986–96) who played 161 games for the blue and golds and captained the side to some great wins, including the outplaying of the Springboks in 1994.

Introduction and Acknowledgements

LISA KINGI

Chief Executive Officer, New Zealand Rugby Foundation

No one ever wants to consider the unimaginable; to permanently lose their mobility due to a rugby accident. But sadly, it does occur. Rugby is a contact sport. Statistically, there are approximately two catastrophic injuries per annum per 100,000 players in New Zealand. We are all committed to actively reducing this.

The New Zealand Rugby Foundation is the first line of support, focusing on 'instant support', and later, as a player rehabilitates, on bridging the gap between the 'before' and 'after' quality of life for these players.

Money can go some way towards making the players' lives easier, but it requires more than that. The impact on the player, his family and those near to him is hard to describe. This is what is so vital about the Foundation: the organisation stands by the player, with camaraderie — for life.

This year we 'celebrate' our twenty-fifth anniversary — quite a milestone. The nature of what we do and our reason to exist causes mixed feelings when we use the word 'celebrate'. However, there are many stories that should be celebrated. We have ninety-four amazing VIPs on our books — yes Very Injured Players and Very Important People!

We would like to acknowledge all of the individuals who have contributed recipes to this book; the step-up from everyone has been heart-warming.

For us at the Foundation this has been a labour of love and even more so to experience the support that we have from the individuals who gave us their time to appear in the photo shoots. We are also hugely grateful to those individuals who gave up their time to appear in the photo shoots: Andy Ellis, Anna Richards, Anthony Boric, Bryan Williams, Charlie Faumuina, Sir Colin Meads, Conrad Smith, Corey Flynn, David Latta, Jamie Mackintosh, Jarrad Hoeata, Jason Rutledge, Jerome Kaino, Jimmy Cowan, Keven Mealamu, Kurt Baker, Mark Ranby, Melodie Robinson, Piri Weepu, Robbie Fruean, Tane Norton, Tom Donnelly, Victor Vito and Waka Nathan. Take a bow!

And extra-special thanks to Conrad Smith and Victor Vito for gracing the front cover. Thanks, guys!

Thank you to the NZRU for their blessing, especially Sam Allen, and also Charlotte Wilson for the individual player biographies. Thanks to the franchise management teams and coaches who accommodated our photo shoots in between busy training schedules, in particular Rachel Martelli, Mark Ranby, Libby Gudmundsson and Peter Sinclair. Thanks to All Black management; Rob Nichol and Dave Gibson of the NZRPA and their player development managers; and the many individual players' agents, especially Tim Castle, Dean Hegan, Simon Porter and Karyne Ross, who worked collectively to help us achieve our goal.

The shoots took place mostly in private homes: our grateful thanks to Kelly Hyde and Shaun McMahon and their daughters Grace and Holly for opening their home to us in Christchurch: 'Oh, the keys are under the mat — just go in and make yourselves at home . . . and shut the door when you're done'; to John, Carmel, Jack and Amaya Leslie (and their gorgeous dog Juno), who did the same in Dunedin; to Chrissie Fernyhough, who allowed us to use

her beautiful home in Auckland; and to Pippa and Tim Park for their gorgeous cottage in Lyall Bay in Wellington. The Kelliher Estate also played a vital role when Grahame Dawson and his team opened the doors to the magnificent homestead and gardens on Puketutu Island, and in addition they have gifted us an opportunity to host a premium fundraising dinner at this exclusive venue.

On behalf of all of us at the Foundation, grateful thanks to Kieran Scott and Melanie Jenkins for their beautiful photography; Kathy Paterson for her incredible food and fun in recipe testing and cooking for the photo shoots; Tam West for her terrific styling; and lastly to Jenny Hellen of Random House for her patience, perseverance, dedication and sheer professionalism in making the book come together.

Enjoy the book — tell your friends, buy a second one! Thank you, it is the unwavering support from rugby lovers and food lovers like you that makes such a difference to this excellent cause.

RUGBY FOUNDATION
www.rugbyfoundation.com

01

Light Meals and Entrées

BUCK ANDERSON'S
Pancakes

MAKES ABOUT
10 PANCAKES

1 cup flour
pinch of salt
2 tablespoons caster sugar
3 eggs
1¼ cups milk
butter for frying
caster sugar or vanilla sugar to serve
lemon juice to serve

Sift the flour with a pinch of salt into a medium-sized bowl. Stir in the sugar and make a well in the centre.

Whisk together the eggs and milk and gradually pour into the well, beating to form a smooth batter. Cover and rest for 30 minutes.

Heat a little butter in an 18 cm or 20 cm frying pan. Pour in enough batter to coat the base of the pan. Cook for 1 minute or until golden brown. Turn the pancake to cook the other side. Keep warm on a plate, under a soft clean tea towel, while cooking the remaining batter.

To serve, sprinkle caster sugar or vanilla sugar and squeeze lemon juice over each pancake, roll up and eat, making sure you cut 2 cm off the end as tax for the cook!

Buck Anderson was an All Blacks lock (1986–87) who played for Wairarapa Bush (1982–87) and Waikato (1989–93), including the Mooloos' epic Ranfurly Shield win in 1993. He is the General Manager for Community and Provincial Union Rugby at the NZRU.

SERVES 6

ANTHONY BORIC'S
Seafood Chowder

12 fresh mussels, scrubbed

1 cup white wine

2 small onions, chopped

2 tablespoons oil

3 rashers rindless bacon, cut into strips

3 potatoes, peeled and cut into 1 cm dice — use a waxy variety

1 cup water

2 cups full-cream milk

4 fillets firm-textured white fish, cut into chunks

200 grams raw prawn cutlets, tail on but shell removed

½ cup cream

2 tablespoons chopped fresh parsley

salt and pepper

Place the mussels into a large pot with the white wine and 1 chopped onion. Place on the lid and bring to the boil over a high heat.

When the wine is boiling, remove the lid and, as each mussel opens and shrinks away from the shell, take it out and let it cool. When all the mussels have opened, strain the cooking liquid and set aside. Remove the mussels from their shells.

Heat the oil in a large saucepan, add the bacon and the remaining chopped onion and cook over a low heat for 5 minutes, until the onion is soft.

Add the potato pieces, water and 1 cup of the reserved mussel cooking liquid. Bring to the boil, lower the heat, cover and simmer for 15 minutes or until the potatoes are tender.

Add the milk, white fish and prawns. Simmer gently for 5 minutes. Stir in the mussels, cream and parsley, simmer for 1 minute and season to taste with salt and pepper.

Serve in warm soup bowls with crusty bread and lemon wedges.

Anthony Boric made his All Blacks debut at lock in 2008. He has represented North Harbour since 2005 and has been part of the Blues since 2006.

MAKES ABOUT
15–20 FRITTERS

DR FARAH PALMER'S
Paua Fritters

FOR THE BATTER

½ cup flour

½ teaspoon baking powder

2 eggs, lightly beaten

2 tablespoons milk, or more if batter
is too thick

salt and pepper

FOR THE PAUA MIXTURE

500 grams paua (shucked weight)

½ cup finely chopped red onion

2 cloves garlic, crushed

½ cup chopped fresh herbs
(coriander, parsley and basil work
well here)

1 tablespoon lemon or lime juice

oil for cooking

lemon wedges to serve

Sift the flour and baking powder into a bowl and make a well in the centre. Pour in the eggs and milk and whisk until smooth. Season with salt and pepper. Cover and place in the refrigerator until ready to use.

For best results, mince the paua with a hand mincer or using the mincer attachment of an electric mixer. Alternatively, dice the paua as finely as you can. Place in a bowl and add the onion, garlic, herbs and lemon or lime juice.

Add the batter to the paua mixture and combine.

Heat a frying pan over a medium heat, add a dash of oil then spoon in the fritter mixture to make fritters of the size you desire. Cook until golden on each side, then place on a platter.

Serve with sliced and buttered fresh white bread and plenty of lemon wedges.

Dr Farah Palmer was a Black Ferns hooker (1996–2006) who captained the team to wins at three Women's Rugby World Cups. She is on the New Zealand Maori Rugby Board, has a PhD in Sociology and was awarded an ONZM in 2007 for services to women's rugby and sport.

SERVES 4

ANDREW ELLIS'
Nacho Dip

FOR THE SALSA
1 avocado, peeled and cut into small
    chunks
2 large ripe tomatoes, deseeded and
    cut into small chunks
1 small red onion, finely chopped
1 small red chilli, deseeded and
    finely chopped
juice of 1 lemon or lime

FOR THE DIP
oil for cooking
450 grams premium beef mince
1 packet of taco seasoning mix
1 cup beef stock
1 x 435 gram can refried beans or
    1 x 400 gram can drained red
    kidney beans
1 x 250 gram tub sour cream
1 cup grated cheese
corn chips to serve

Combine the salsa ingredients in a small bowl and set aside.

Lightly oil a medium-sized ovenproof dish. Heat a dash of oil in a frying pan and cook the mince until it is lightly browned. Add taco seasoning mix to taste, moisten with the stock and place in the ovenproof dish. Warm the refried or kidney beans and place on top of the mince.

Preheat the grill. Spoon over the sour cream. Place the salsa on top, sprinkle over grated cheese and place under the preheated grill until the cheese melts. Get a bag of corn chips and go to town on the dish. A couple of beers will go down a treat as well.

Andrew Ellis made his All Blacks debut at halfback in 2006, the same year he made his Super Rugby debut for the Crusaders and a year after he first played for Canterbury. He also played for New Zealand Under 21 (2005) and the Junior All Blacks (2007).

ALBERT NIKORO'S

Teriyaki Chicken Avocado Sushi

SERVES 4

FOR THE TERIYAKI CHICKEN

200 grams chicken breast, skinned
   and cut into 2 cm pieces
1 tablespoon mirin
1 tablespoon light soy sauce
1 tablespoon vegetable oil
½ teaspoon cornflour
1 tablespoon water

FOR THE RICE

2 cups sushi rice
¼ cup rice vinegar
2 teaspoons sugar
¼ teaspoon salt

TO ASSEMBLE

4 sheets nori
8 slices avocado

TO SERVE

soy sauce
wasabi
pickled ginger

Place the chicken pieces in a bowl with the mirin and soy sauce. Cover and place in the refrigerator to marinate for 1 hour.

Heat a large frying pan, add the oil and pan-fry the chicken pieces for 3 minutes or until cooked through. Mix the cornflour with the water and stir through the cooked chicken. Transfer to a plate and leave the chicken to cool completely.

Wash the rice in cold water and drain well. Place in a heavy-based saucepan and add cold water to cover the rice up to the first knuckle of your index finger when touching the rice with the tip of your finger. Bring to the boil and cover. Reduce the heat and simmer for 20 minutes. Turn off the heat and let stand for a further 10 minutes. Place the cooked rice in a large shallow bowl.

Place the vinegar in a small saucepan and bring to the boil over a high heat. Add the sugar and salt and stir to combine. Reduce the heat to low and cook for a further 2 minutes. Allow to cool before using.

Pour the vinegar mixture into the rice. Using a rice paddle or wooden spoon, 'cut' the rice gently with a slicing motion, making sure all the grains are seasoned with the vinegar mixture. Try not to over-mix or the rice will become mushy.

To assemble, place 1 sheet of nori shiny side down on a clean, dry chopping board or sushi-rolling mat. Place a quarter of the sushi rice over the half of the nori that is closest to you. In the centre of the rice, make a line of cooked chicken pieces and avocado slices. Use your thumbs to lift the edge of the nori that is closest to you, keeping the filling in place with your fingers. Roll the edge of the nori away from you into a tight cylinder (as you would a Swiss roll). Seal the edge with a little water. Repeat the process to make 3 more rolls. Using a sharp knife, slice each roll into 6 pieces and serve with soy sauce, wasabi and pickled ginger.

Albert Nikoro debuted for the Blues in 2012. The outside back has also appeared in black as part of the New Zealand Schools and New Zealand Under 17 sides and New Zealand Under 20 training squad.

SERVES 4

PITA ALATINI'S
Tuna or Salmon Sashimi

FOR THE DIPPING SAUCE

1½ tablespoons mirin

3 teaspoons saké

½ cup light soy sauce

½ teaspoon dashi granules (optional)

TO ASSEMBLE

10 cm piece of daikon radish, peeled

500 grams sashimi-grade tuna or
salmon, preferably cut into large
batons, roughly 5 cm square at the
ends

5 cm piece of fresh ginger, peeled
and very finely grated

Pour the mirin and saké into a small saucepan and bring to the boil. Turn off the heat and add the soy sauce and dashi granules, if using. Mix well and set aside. Alternatively, you can just use tamari soy sauce as a dipping sauce.

Cut the daikon radish into a square using a very sharp knife then slice it into very thin slices (use a mandoline if you have one). Stack the slices on top of each other and slice into very thin sticks. Place the daikon radish sticks in a bowl of ice-cold water and toss them until they are all separated.

Slice the tuna or salmon into thin slices, cutting against the grain.

To assemble, dry off the daikon radish sticks and arrange on the plates. Place slices of the cut tuna on top. Now, if you want to be really fancy, mound the grated ginger into little cones and place on each plate. Garnish with edible greens, such as Italian parsley, mint leaves, very finely sliced spring onion or finely sliced cucumber, if using.

To eat, mix a little of the ginger into the dipping sauce or soy sauce then pick up the tuna with chopsticks. Eat the daikon radish sticks in between bites of tuna.

It is traditional to drink saké with sashimi, but you could also have a pilsner beer or crisp white wine.

Pita Alatini was a second five-eighth for the New Zealand Colts (1997), New Zealand Academy (1997–87) and All Blacks (1999–2001). He played Super Rugby for the Crusaders (1996), Chiefs (1997), Highlanders (1998–2001) and Hurricanes (2002–03) and provincial rugby for Southland, Otago and Wellington.

ANNA RICHARDS'

Camembert and Fig Bread Plait

SERVES 4–6

500 grams high-grade flour

1½ teaspoons salt

1 teaspoon sugar

1½ teaspoons active dry yeast

1¼ cups tepid water

3 tablespoons fig chutney, or similar

60 grams camembert cheese, cut into even-sized small pieces

olive oil for brushing

Sift the flour and salt into a large bowl. Place the sugar in a small ramekin or bowl, sprinkle over the yeast and pour in about a third of the tepid water. Set aside for 5 minutes for the yeast to froth. Make a well in the centre of the flour and pour in the remaining tepid water and the yeast mixture.

Begin mixing with a large wooden spoon or fork, or just use the fingertips of one hand (keep the other clean to answer the phone!), until the dough comes together. Tip the soft dough out on to a lightly floured bench and begin to knead by turning, folding and pushing with the heel of your hand. Continue to knead for 10–15 minutes until the dough is smooth, shiny and elastic.

Place the dough in a large, lightly oiled bowl. Turn dough over to oil the surface, which prevents a skin forming, and cover the bowl with plastic wrap. Leave in a warm place for at least 1 hour or until the dough has doubled in size. Timing will depend on how warm or cold your kitchen is. Preheat the oven to 200°C. Line a baking tray with baking paper.

Tip the dough back out on to a lightly floured bench and roll it out to a 25 cm x 25 cm square. Spread the fig chutney on to the rolled dough and dot with the pieces of camembert cheese, patting them down with the palm of your hand. Roll up the dough tightly to form a Swiss roll or pinwheel. Pinch the dough to seal the edge. Using a sharp knife, make a single lengthways cut down the middle of the roll, all the way through the dough. With the cut side of each dough strand facing up, twist the two strands around each other. Place the plait on the lined tray and press the ends together firmly. Cover the dough with floured plastic wrap and leave to rise until the plait has doubled in size.

Place the plait in the preheated oven and bake for 20–25 minutes until well browned. (If you tap the base of the bread it should sound hollow.) Remove the bread plait from the oven and brush with olive oil.

Serve sliced with extra cheese and chutney.

Anna Richards was a first five-eighth who made her Black Ferns debut in 1990 and retired in 2010 as the most-capped Black Fern ever and winner of four Women's Rugby World Cups. She was also a national Touch representative and Sevens player and won numerous provincial rugby titles with Auckland.

SERVES 4

BEN CASTLE'S
Seafood Chowder

knob of butter

3 rashers rindless bacon, cut into
  strips

1 onion, finely chopped

1 leek, white part only, finely sliced

2 tablespoons flour

600 ml full-cream milk

100 ml fish stock

400 grams potatoes, peeled and cut
  into 1–2 cm dice

½ cup frozen sweetcorn or canned
  sweetcorn kernels, drained

½ cup frozen green peas

150 grams white fish fillets, cut into
  large chunks (I like to use tarakihi)

200 grams salmon fillets, cut into
  large chunks

12 scallops

12 raw prawn cutlets, tail on and
  shell removed

salt and freshly ground black pepper

1 tablespoon chopped fresh parsley
  to serve (optional)

smoked paprika to serve (optional)

Place a knob of butter in a large saucepan, add the bacon and cook over a medium heat until the bacon begins to brown. Lower the heat, add the onion and leek and cook for 10 minutes or until the leek is soft. Sprinkle over the flour, mix well and cook for a further minute.

Pour in the milk, stirring continuously to avoid any lumps. Add the fish stock and potatoes. Bring to the boil then lower the heat to a simmer and cook for 10 minutes, stirring occasionally. Add the sweetcorn and peas and cook for a further 2 minutes. Add the seafood and simmer gently for 5 minutes or until the seafood is just cooked. Season to taste with salt and pepper.

Ladle the seafood chowder into warmed soup bowls and sprinkle with the chopped parsley and smoked paprika if desired.

Serve with plenty of crusty bread and an ice-cold beer. Cheers!

Ben Castle was an Otago (2002) and Bay of Plenty prop (2003–07) who played for New Zealand Universities and the Junior All Blacks (2005). He played for the Chiefs (2004–08) and Western Force (2009) in Super Rugby and for Toulon (2008–09) and Newport Gwent Dragons (2009–12) in the north.

SERVES 2

RICHARD KAHUI'S
Sweet Chilli Mussels

12–14 fresh mussels in the shell, scrubbed and de-bearded
500 ml cream
1 tablespoon sweet chilli sauce
2 cloves garlic, crushed

Place the mussels in a large saucepan with the cream, sweet chilli sauce and garlic.

Place the lid on top and bring to the boil. Remove the lid and, as each mussel opens and shrinks away from the shell, take it out and place it into serving bowls. Discard any mussels that do not open.

When all the mussels have opened, pour over the sauce and enjoy — it's awesome!

Serve with sliced baguette to mop up all those juices.

Richard Kahui made his All Blacks debut at centre in 2008. His representative career includes New Zealand Under 16 (2001), Under 17 (2002), Under 19 (2003–04) and Under 21 (2005–06) as well as New Zealand Maori. He has played for Waikato since 2004, the Chiefs since 2007 and the Highlanders (2006).

02

KICK OFF

Pasta and Risotto

SERVES 6

DAN CARTER'S

Lasagne

Aaron Cruden and Zac Guildford are also keen lasagne cooks.

FOR THE BOLOGNESE SAUCE

2 tablespoons olive oil

2 medium-sized onions, chopped

2 cloves garlic, crushed

1 kilogram premium beef mince

2 x 400 gram cans tomato purée or
    bottled tomato passata

1 cup beef stock

¼ cup chopped fresh Italian parsley

salt and freshly ground black pepper

FOR THE WHITE SAUCE

75 grams butter

4 tablespoons flour

3 cups milk

¾ cup freshly grated parmesan
    cheese

TO ASSEMBLE

300 grams fresh lasagne sheets, cut
    to fit if necessary

¾ cup grated mozzarella cheese

To prepare the Bolognese sauce heat a large, deep frying pan over a medium heat. Add the olive oil and onions and cook for 10 minutes. Stir in the garlic and cook for 1 minute. Add the mince and cook, stirring continuously to break it up, until the mince begins to brown and any liquid evaporates. Add the tomato purée and stock and cook for 20 minutes until the sauce has thickened. Stir through the parsley and season with salt and pepper. Set aside while you make the white sauce.

Melt the butter in a heavy-based saucepan. Add the flour and stir over a low heat for 2 minutes to cook the flour. Remove the pan from the heat and pour in the milk, stirring continuously to avoid lumps. Return to the heat and cook, stirring continuously until the sauce is thick and shiny. Season with salt and pepper. Remove from the heat and stir through the parmesan cheese or, if not using immediately, sprinkle the cheese over the surface of the white sauce to prevent a skin from forming.

Preheat the oven to 190°C. Grease a 20 cm x 20 cm square ovenproof dish or similar. Place a shallow baking tray in the oven to catch any spillage from the cooking lasagne. Line the base of the dish with a lasagne sheet. Spoon over half of the Bolognese sauce and cover with a lasagne sheet. Spoon over half of the white sauce and cover with a lasagne sheet. Spoon over the remaining Bolognese sauce, cover with a lasagne sheet and finish with the remaining white sauce. Sprinkle with the mozzarella cheese.

Cook in the preheated oven for 25–30 minutes until the top is golden and the lasagne is bubbling hot. Serve with a simple salad.

Dan Carter debuted for the All Blacks in 2003, a year after playing for New Zealand Under 21. One of rugby's best first five-eighths, he holds the current record for most Test points by any international player and has won multiple Super Rugby titles with the Crusaders.

Aaron Cruden made his All Blacks debut in 2010 against Ireland. The first five-eighth, who captained New Zealand Under 20 and was IRB Junior Player of the Year in 2009 and ITM Cup Player of the year in 2011, has played for Manawatu since 2008 and made his Super Rugby debut in 2010.

Zac Guildford earned All Blacks selection at wing in 2009, the same year in which he was part of the Junior World Championship-winning New Zealand Under 20 side for the second time. He plays for Hawke's Bay (since 2007) and the Crusaders (since 2010).

SERVES 4

ALEX BRADLEY'S

Surf 'n' Turf Penne

400 grams penne

50 grams butter

400 grams chicken breast, skinned
and cut into strips

salt and freshly ground black pepper

12 raw prawn cutlets, tail on and
shell removed

130 grams washed baby spinach
(about 1 packet)

½ cup milk

2 tablespoons cream

1 punnet of cherry tomatoes

¾–1 cup freshly grated parmesan
cheese

Cook the penne in a large saucepan of boiling salted water for 10 minutes, until al dente, or according to the instructions on the packet. Drain, rinse under a little cold water to arrest cooking, and set aside while you make the sauce.

Place half the butter in a large, deep-sided frying pan over a medium heat and cook the chicken strips for about 5 minutes, turning once. Season with salt and pepper and set aside on a plate.

Place the raw prawns in the pan and cook until they just turn pink. Remove and set aside with the cooked chicken.

Add the remaining butter to the frying pan, then the spinach and cook until it just begins to wilt. Stir in the milk and cream and cook for 1–2 minutes. Return the chicken and prawns to the frying pan with the penne, toss through the cherry tomatoes and cook until hot. Stir through the parmesan cheese.

Place in a warm serving bowl. Serve with extra grated parmesan and pass around the pepper grinder.

Alex Bradley made his Super Rugby debut for the Chiefs in 2012 after three strong seasons at number 8 for Waikato.

KIERAN READ'S

Smoked Chicken and Chive Fettuccine

SERVES 4

400 grams fresh fettuccine

1 tablespoon olive oil

25 grams butter

4 spring onions, sliced

4 cloves garlic, crushed

1 cup chicken stock

150 ml cream

1 tablespoon wholegrain mustard

2 smoked chicken breasts, meat pulled apart into strips

2 tablespoons snipped or chopped chives

salt and pepper

Cook the fettuccine in a large saucepan of lightly salted boiling water for 3–5 minutes or until al dente. Drain well and toss through the olive oil to prevent the pasta from sticking.

Melt the butter in a large frying pan and add the spring onions and garlic. Cook until soft but not coloured, about 5 minutes. Stir in the chicken stock, cream and mustard. Bring just to the boil, reduce the heat and simmer until it reaches a sauce consistency.

Add the smoked chicken and cooked pasta to the sauce and cook until hot. Stir through the chives, season with salt and pepper, and serve.

Kieran Read made his All Blacks debut at number 8 in 2008 after pulling on the black jersey for New Zealand Schools (2003), Under 19 (2004), Under 21 (2005–06) and the Junior All Blacks (2007). He has played for Canterbury since 2006 and the Crusaders since 2007.

TOM DONNELLY'S
Chilli and Lime Prawn Pasta

SERVES 4

400 grams fresh spaghetti

3 tablespoons olive oil

16–20 large raw prawns, shelled and deveined

2 cloves garlic, crushed

1 red chilli, deseeded and finely chopped

4 spring onions, trimmed and sliced

½ cup white wine

15 grams butter

4 ripe tomatoes, chopped

zest and juice of 2 limes

salt and freshly ground black pepper

½ cup freshly grated parmesan cheese shavings

Bring a large saucepan of lightly salted water to the boil. Drop in the spaghetti and cook for 4 minutes or until al dente. Drain, rinse under cold water and drain again. Toss through 1 tablespoon of olive oil to prevent the spaghetti from sticking. Set aside.

Heat the remaining 2 tablespoons of olive oil in a large frying pan. Add the prawns and cook for 2 minutes. Add the garlic, chilli and spring onions and cook for a further 2 minutes. Pour in the white wine and allow to bubble up and reduce. Add the butter, tomatoes and lime zest and juice. Toss through the spaghetti until all is well combined and heated through. Season with salt and pepper.

Serve with the parmesan cheese and chopped parsley, if using.

Tom Donnelly earned All Blacks selection at lock in 2009 and 2010. He has enjoyed a long career with Otago since making his debut in 2002 and joined the Crusaders in 2012 after playing for the Highlanders (2004–11).

SERVES 4
AS A SIDE DISH

MARK RANBY'S

Roasted Pumpkin and Feta Risotto

2 cups peeled and diced (2 cm)
   pumpkin
2 tablespoons olive oil
salt and pepper
25 grams butter
1 onion, finely chopped
2 cloves garlic, finely chopped
1 cup arborio rice
½ cup white wine
3 cups hot chicken stock
100 grams marinated feta cheese
8 sage leaves pan-fried in 1
   tablespoon hot olive oil until crisp
   to garnish (optional)
parmesan cheese, grated to garnish
   (optional)

Preheat the oven to 190°C.

Lay the pumpkin pieces flat on a baking tray, pour over 1 tablespoon of the olive oil, season with salt and pepper and cook for 10 minutes. Turn the pumpkin pieces over and cook for a further 10 minutes or until the pumpkin is cooked. Set aside.

Heat the remaining tablespoon of oil and the butter in a wide saucepan, add the onion and cook gently until soft but not coloured, about 10 minutes. Add the garlic and cook for a further minute. Add the rice, stirring to coat with the oil, then add the wine and stir until all the liquid has evaporated. Add the hot chicken stock a ladleful at a time, stirring continuously until all the liquid is absorbed before you add the next ladleful. Keep the risotto at a rapid simmer. Continue adding the stock until the rice is al dente, about 20 minutes, but start checking after 15 minutes.

Add the marinated feta and fold through the roasted pumpkin. Season with salt and pepper to taste and garnish with fried sage leaves and parmesan cheese, if you wish.

I love serving this dish with lamb shanks or a venison steak.

Mark Ranby played at second five-eighth for New Zealand Schools (1995), Colts (1997–98) and the All Blacks (2001). He played Super Rugby for the Hurricanes (1997) and Chiefs (1998–2005) as well as provincial rugby for Manawatu and Waikato. He is the Crusaders' Professional Development Manager.

SERVES 4
AS AN ENTRÉE
OR SIDE DISH

WAYNE SMITH'S
Mushroom Risotto

3 tablespoons olive oil

500 grams fresh mushrooms, sliced

salt and freshly ground black pepper

50 grams butter

1 onion, finely chopped

2 cloves garlic, finely chopped

1 cup arborio rice

½ cup white wine

3 cups hot chicken or vegetable stock
   (more if needed)

¼ cup freshly grated parmesan
   cheese

lemon juice to taste

½ cup fresh Italian parsley, coarsely
   chopped

Heat 2 tablespoons of the olive oil in a frying pan. Cook the mushrooms in batches over a medium heat until the mushrooms have coloured and the liquid has evaporated. Season with salt and pepper. Set aside.

Heat half the butter and the remaining olive oil in a wide saucepan, add the onion and cook gently until soft but not coloured, about 10 minutes. Add the garlic and cook for a further 2 minutes. Add the rice, stirring to coat with the oil, and cook for 1–2 minutes. Then add the wine and stir until all the liquid has evaporated. Add a ladleful of hot stock at a time, stirring continuously until all the liquid is absorbed. Then add the next ladleful. The risotto should be kept at a rapid simmer. Continue adding the stock until the rice is al dente (about 20 minutes) but start checking after 15 minutes.

Add the remaining butter, parmesan cheese and lemon juice, and stir well. Add the cooked mushrooms and Italian parsley.

Serve with extra parmesan cheese if you wish.

Wayne Smith was an All Blacks first five-eighth (1980–85), Head Coach (2000–01) and Assistant Coach (2004–11) who was part of the team that won RWC 2011. He won two titles as Coach of the Crusaders (1997–99), coached the Northampton Saints and in 2012 became Assistant Coach of the Chiefs.

SERVES 4

JAMIE JOSEPH'S
Crayfish Spaghetti

1 live crayfish

2 tablespoons olive oil

1 onion, chopped

2 cloves garlic, peeled

1 carrot, peeled and sliced

1 stick celery, sliced

½ cup white wine

2 x 400 gram cans chopped tomatoes
  in juice

1 tablespoon tomato paste

salt and pepper

400 grams dried spaghetti

¼ cup chopped fresh parsley

¼ cup freshly grated parmesan
  cheese

knob of butter

Drown the crayfish in fresh water. With a sharp knife, split the crayfish down the centre from the head to the tail. Remove the guts from the head cavity and the excretion tube that runs down through to the tail. Separate the head and all the shell to make the stock.

Place the olive oil, onion, garlic, carrot and celery in a saucepan over a medium heat and cook for 10 minutes. Add the wine, tomatoes, tomato paste and season with salt and pepper. Lay the crayfish head and shell on top, and bring to the boil. Lower the heat and simmer gently for 1 hour.

Sieve the crayfish stock, pressing down on the vegetables to extract all the flavour. Place the sieved stock back into the saucepan and reduce to a sauce consistency if necessary.

Meanwhile, cook the spaghetti in lightly salted boiling water according to the directions on the packet, or until al dente. Drain the spaghetti and place into the sauce, stirring through the parsley and parmesan cheese.

Add a knob of butter to a hot frying pan and sear the crayfish tail meat until the meat is no longer transparent. Remove from the frying pan and slice.

Place the spaghetti on serving plates and top with the crayfish. Serve with extra parmesan if you wish and pass around the pepper grinder.

Jamie Joseph played at flanker for Otago (1989–95), New Zealand Colts (1989), New Zealand Maori (1991–95) and the All Blacks (1992–95). He has coached Wellington (2007–10), New Zealand Maori (2010) and the Highlanders (since 2011).

SERVES 4

OWEN FRANKS'

Macaroni Cheese

2 cups dried macaroni

50 grams butter

3 tablespoons flour

3 cups milk

½ cup cream

1 cup grated cheddar cheese

salt

½ cup panko or dried breadcrumbs

extra ½ cup grated cheddar for
  topping

Preheat the oven to 200°C. Lightly grease an ovenproof dish.

Cook the macaroni in lightly salted boiling water according to the instructions on the packet, or until al dente. Drain and rinse under cold water to arrest the cooking, and set aside while making the sauce.

In a medium-sized saucepan, melt the butter over a low heat then stir in the flour to form a roux. Allow the roux to bubble gently, stirring continuously until lightly golden. Add the milk and cream to the roux, about one cup at a time. Stir or whisk continuously, until all the milk and cream have been added and the sauce is thick enough to coat the back of a wooden spoon. Stir in the grated cheddar, and season with salt to taste. Stir the cooked macaroni through the cheese sauce.

Spoon into the greased dish and top with the panko crumbs or breadcrumbs and extra grated cheese.

Place in the preheated oven and cook for 15–20 minutes until golden and bubbling. Serve with thick slices of ham off the bone or crusty bread and your favourite chutney.

Owen Franks made his All Blacks debut in 2009, just a few months after making his Super Rugby debut for the Crusaders. A powerful prop, his representative career also includes appearances for New Zealand Schools and New Zealand Under 21.

SERVES 4

DOUG TIETJENS'

Chicken and Bacon Fettuccine

2 tablespoons olive oil

400 grams chicken breast, skinned and cut into strips

4 rashers rindless bacon or chicken bacon, cut into strips

1 onion, finely chopped

250 grams mushrooms, sliced

1 cup chicken stock

½ cup cream

400 grams fresh fettuccine

130 grams washed baby spinach (about 1 packet)

salt and freshly ground black pepper

Heat 1 tablespoon of the oil in a frying pan and cook the chicken strips over a medium-high heat for 5 minutes, turning once. Transfer to a plate and set aside.

Place the remaining tablespoon of oil in the pan and cook the bacon and onion for about 5 minutes. Add the mushrooms and cook for a further 4 minutes, stirring occasionally.

Pour the chicken stock into the pan and allow to bubble up, then add the cream and simmer until the stock and cream thicken to a sauce consistency. Return the chicken to the pan.

Meanwhile, cook the pasta in a large saucepan of boiling salted water for 3–5 minutes, until al dente, or following the instructions on the packet. Drain well, reserving some of the cooking water if you need to thin the sauce. Drop the cooked fettuccine and baby spinach leaves into the sauce and season with salt and pepper. Toss well and serve in warmed pasta bowls.

Doug Tietjens has played at loose forward for Manawatu since 2008 and made his Super Rugby debut in 2012 for the Highlanders.

SERVES 2

SIR JOHN GRAHAM'S
Sunday Night Pasta

1 teaspoon chicken or vegetable
   stock powder
200 grams pasta, such as orecchiette,
   penne or fusilli
1 tablespoon olive oil
2–3 rashers rindless bacon, diced
1 onion, chopped
2 red capsicums, or a mixture of red,
   yellow and green, deseeded and
   diced or cut into strips
½ cup sour cream
freshly grated parmesan cheese to
   serve (optional)

Bring a large saucepan of lightly salted water to the boil and add the chicken or vegetable stock powder. Add the pasta and cook until al dente, about 10 minutes, or according to the instructions on the packet. Drain the pasta using a large sieve into a heatproof jug, reserving the cooking water. Splash the olive oil over the pasta.

Place the bacon and onion into a large frying pan and cook over a low heat until golden. Increase the heat and add the diced capsicum and cook for 2–3 minutes or until the capsicum just begins to soften.

Toss through the cooked pasta with about ½ cup of the reserved cooking water to moisten. Stir through the sour cream and serve with the parmesan cheese, if using.

Alternatively, you can roast the capsicums in advance, even the day before. Preheat the oven to 200°C. Remove the green stems and cores from the capsicums and wash well to remove the white seeds inside, then dry. Place in a shallow roasting dish lined with baking paper and roast until the skin is well blistered, turning once, 25–30 minutes. Allow to cool before peeling off and discarding the skin. Cut the flesh into slices.

Sir John Graham was an All Blacks loose forward (1958–64) and was knighted in 2011 for services to education and sports. He played for Auckland (1955–57), Canterbury (1958–65) and New Zealand Universities (1957) and is a past President of the NZRU.

03

Pies

SERVES 4

BG WILLIAMS'
Tuna Pie

FOR THE POTATOES

3 large floury potatoes, peeled and
   cut into pieces
½ cup hot milk
salt and pepper

FOR THE SAUCE

50 grams butter
1 small onion, finely chopped
3 tablespoons flour
2 cups milk

FOR THE FILLING AND CRUST

4 eggs, boiled for 8 minutes, peeled
   and quartered
1 x 425 gram can chunky-style tuna
   in spring water, drained
1 cup grated tasty cheddar cheese
½ cup panko or dried white
   breadcrumbs

Preheat the oven to 190°C. Grease a 4-cup capacity ovenproof dish or 4 individual ovenproof dishes.

Boil the potatoes in plenty of lightly salted water until soft. Drain, dry off over the heat and mash. Beat in the hot milk, season with salt and pepper and set aside.

Melt the butter in a medium-sized saucepan, add the onion and cook over a low heat for 5 minutes until soft. Add the flour and cook for a further 2 minutes, stirring continuously. Gradually pour in the milk and stir well to combine. Cook until the sauce is thick and creamy, 10–15 minutes. Season with salt and pepper to taste.

Mix the mashed potato into the sauce and carefully fold through the eggs and tuna. Spoon into the prepared ovenproof dish. Combine the cheese and breadcrumbs and sprinkle evenly over the top. Cook in the preheated oven for 20 minutes or until golden and bubbling hot. Serve with wedges of lemon, if you wish, and pass around the pepper grinder.

BG Williams was an All Blacks (1970–78) and Auckland (1968–82) wing who played well over 250 first class matches. He has coached Auckland and Manu Samoa and was Assistant Coach at the Hurricanes. In 2011 he was elected President of the NZRU.

SERVES 4

JASON EMERY'S

Shepherd's Pie

1 tablespoon vegetable oil
1 onion, finely chopped
500 grams premium lamb or beef
  mince
1 x 400 gram can chopped tomatoes
  in juice
½ cup lamb or beef stock
3–4 drops Worcestershire sauce
salt and pepper
½–1 cup mixed frozen vegetables

FOR THE TOPPING
3 large floury potatoes
½ cup hot milk
25 grams butter
½ cup grated cheddar cheese
  (optional)

Preheat the oven to 190°C. Lightly grease a 4-cup capacity pie dish or similar ovenproof dish.

Place the oil and onion in a saucepan and cook over a low heat until the onion is soft, about 5 minutes. Add the mince, turn up the heat and cook for 5 minutes, stirring until the mince begins to brown. Add the tomatoes, stock and Worcestershire sauce, and season with salt and pepper. Simmer, covered, for 20 minutes then uncover and add the frozen vegetables. Cook for a further 10–15 minutes or until most of the liquid has evaporated.

Meanwhile, place the potatoes in a large saucepan with lightly salted water to cover and boil until tender, about 20 minutes. Drain, then dry off over the heat, shaking the saucepan until the potatoes appear dry. Mash the potatoes then thoroughly beat in the hot milk and butter.

Place the cooked mince in the prepared dish. Spoon the mashed potato on top and sprinkle with grated cheddar cheese, if using.

Place in the preheated oven and cook for 20–25 minutes until the potato is golden brown.

Jason Emery was part of the New Zealand Under 20 side that made the final of the Junior World Championship in 2012 and scored three tries at the tournament. He made his provincial rugby debut for Manawatu in 2011.

KURT BAKER'S

Mince and Cheese Pies

MAKES 12

1 onion, finely chopped

oil for cooking

500 grams premium beef mince

¼ cup beef stock

salt and pepper

100 grams cheddar cheese, cut into
small pieces

3 sheets frozen butter puff pastry,
defrosted

1 egg, lightly beaten with a little milk

tomato sauce to serve

Preheat the oven to 190°C. Lightly grease a large baking tray.

In a large frying pan over a low heat, cook the onion in a dash of oil for 5 minutes. Increase the heat, add the mince and cook until browned. Stir in the beef stock and season with salt and pepper. Cook until the stock has been absorbed. Set aside to cool then stir through the cheddar cheese pieces.

Cut each sheet of pre-rolled pastry into 4 squares. Working with 1 pastry square at a time, brush the edges with the beaten egg. Place 3 tablespoons of the mince filling onto one side then fold the pastry over to form a packet. Crimp the edges with a fork to seal. Cut a small slit in the top of the pie to vent steam. Place on the prepared tray and repeat with the remaining pastry squares.

Brush the tops with the beaten egg to glaze. Chill for 10 minutes to allow the pastry to firm up.

Cook in the preheated oven for 20 minutes until golden. Serve with tomato sauce.

Kurt Baker made his New Zealand Sevens debut in 2008 and was part of the squad that won a gold medal at the 2010 Commonwealth Games in Delhi. He was also part of the Junior World Championship-winning New Zealand Under 20 side in 2008 and made his Super Rugby debut for the Highlanders in 2012.

SERVES 4

NICK CROSSWELL'S
Chicken Pie

Jason Rutledge also makes a mean chicken pie.

2 tablespoons vegetable oil

500 grams chicken thighs, boned and skinned, cut into 3 cm pieces

1 onion, finely chopped

1 clove garlic, crushed

1 stick celery, sliced

1 small red capsicum, deseeded and diced

250 grams button mushrooms, quartered

1 x 37 gram packet mushroom soup mix

1 x 37 gram packet creamy chicken soup mix

2 cups water

1 teaspoon Dijon mustard

¼ cup cream or sour cream

2 tablespoons chopped fresh parsley

2 sheets frozen butter puff pastry, defrosted

1 egg, lightly beaten with a pinch of salt

1 teaspoon dried oregano

Heat 1 tablespoon of the oil in a large frying pan over a medium-high heat and brown the chicken pieces on all sides. Remove and set aside on a plate.

Lower the heat slightly, add the remaining oil and then the onion, garlic, celery, capsicum and mushrooms. Cook for 5 minutes then return the browned chicken to the frying pan.

In a bowl, combine the soup mixes with the water and mustard. Pour into the frying pan, stirring continuously, until the mixture begins to thicken. Lower the heat to a simmer and cook for 10 minutes or until the chicken is just cooked. The mixture should be very thick. Add the cream or sour cream and parsley, stirring well to combine. Remove from the heat and allow to cool.

Preheat the oven to 200°C.

On a lightly floured benchtop place the pastry sheets, one on the top of the other, and roll out to fit the shape of a 4-cup capacity pie dish. If you have one, place a pie bird or upturned egg cup in the centre of the pie dish to prevent the pastry going soggy. (The beak of a pie bird allows steam to escape as well.)

Spoon the cooled chicken mixture into the pie dish. Wet the edges of the pie dish with water and place the pastry lid on the dish. Press down firmly with your fingertips to seal, and trim the excess pastry with a sharp knife. Brush the top of the pastry with the egg wash and with a small knife cut 2 slits in the top to allow steam to escape during baking. Sprinkle over the dried oregano.

Bake in the preheated oven for 20–25 minutes or until the pastry is crisp and golden brown in colour and the filling is very hot.

Nick Crosswell has earned over 50 caps as a loose forward for Manawatu since he made his debut in 2006. He made his Super Rugby debut for the Hurricanes in 2010 and joined the Highlanders in 2011.
Jason Rutledge has been playing first class rugby since 2000, when he made his debut at hooker for Southland. He made his Super Rugby debut in 2004 earned over 50 caps with the Highlanders.

ROSS KENNEDY'S

Pumpkin, Kumara and Pinenut Quiche

SERVES 6

400 gram block frozen savoury
  shortcrust pastry, defrosted
1 cup peeled and diced (2 cm)
  pumpkin
1 cup peeled and diced (2 cm)
  orange kumara
olive oil for cooking
4 rashers rindless bacon, cut into
  strips
1 onion, chopped
¼ cup pinenuts
1 large bunch spinach, washed and
  stems removed
100 grams feta cheese
5 eggs
250 ml milk, or ½ milk and ½ cream
salt and pepper

Preheat the oven to 200°C. Place a baking tray in the oven to heat.

On a lightly floured benchtop, roll out the pastry to 3 mm thickness and press into a 20 cm diameter x 4 cm deep loose-bottomed flan tin. Place in the refrigerator and chill for 20–30 minutes.

Meanwhile, prepare the filling by cooking the pumpkin and kumara in lightly salted water until just tender, about 10 minutes. Drain and set aside.

In a frying pan, heat a dash of oil and cook the bacon, onion and pinenuts until lightly coloured. Transfer to a plate and set aside.

Place the spinach, with the water still clinging to its leaves, in the frying pan and wilt. Remove from the pan and roughly chop.

Remove the pastry case from the refrigerator, line with crumpled baking paper and fill this with uncooked rice or blind-baking beans. Place the tin on the preheated baking tray and bake the pastry for 15 minutes. Remove the paper and rice and return to the oven for a further 5 minutes until the pastry is well cooked and golden.

Lower the oven temperature to 180°C.

Spread the cooked pumpkin and kumara over the base of the cooked pastry case then add the spinach. Crumble the feta over the top.

In a jug, whisk together the eggs and milk, and season with salt and pepper. Carefully pour over the vegetables and feta.

Cook in the preheated oven for 30–35 minutes or until golden and set. Stand for 10 minutes before topping with the bacon mixture and serving with a crisp green salad.

Ross Kennedy has earned close to 100 provincial rugby caps, playing for Wellington (2002–05), Counties Manukau (2006), Otago (2007–08) and Hawke's Bay (2009–10). He played for the Highlanders in 2009, Eastern Province (2011) and joined the Crusaders squad in 2012.

SERVES 6

TANE NORTON'S
Bacon and Egg Pie

2 sheets frozen butter puff pastry,
   defrosted
oil for cooking
4 rashers rindless bacon, cut into
   strips
1 onion, finely chopped
4 bunches fresh spinach, washed
   and stems removed
5 eggs
300 ml cream
salt and pepper
4 small tomatoes, deseeded and
   coarsely chopped
1 tablespoon chutney
½ cup grated cheese

Preheat the oven to 190°C. Place a baking tray in the oven to heat. Lightly flour the benchtop, place 1 sheet of pastry on top of the other and roll out to fit a 20 cm diameter x 4 cm deep fluted pie tin. Ease the pastry into the tin and refrigerate for 20 minutes until firm. Alternatively, use savoury shortcrust pastry and bake blind following the instructions on page 74.

Heat a dash of oil in a frying pan, add the bacon and onion and cook over a low heat for 5 minutes until the onion is soft. Remove to a plate and set aside to cool. Place the spinach, with the water still clinging to its leaves, in the pan and toss with a wooden spoon until the spinach has just begun to wilt. Leave to cool, squeeze out any excess moisture and chop coarsely.

Lightly beat the eggs with the cream and season with salt and pepper to taste. Add the bacon and onion mixture, the chopped spinach and the tomatoes.

Spread the chutney over the pastry base. Pour in the egg mixture and sprinkle with the grated cheese. Place in the preheated oven and cook for 40 minutes or until set and golden.

04

TRY

Seafood and Poultry

SERVES 4

WAKA NATHAN'S
Fish Supreme

1 tablespoon olive oil
1 small onion, finely chopped
2 cloves garlic, crushed
1 green chilli, deseeded and finely
  chopped
1 x 400 gram can chopped tomatoes
  with herbs
⅓ cup white wine
1 red capsicum, deseeded and finely
  diced
1 cup frozen peas
1 large bunch spinach, washed,
  stems removed and leaves torn
  into pieces
500–600 grams firm white fish
  fillets, cut into chunks
250 grams raw prawn cutlets, tail
  shell removed
1 cup cooked rice
salt and pepper

Heat the oil in a large, wide saucepan, add the onion and cook until soft, about 5 minutes. Add the garlic and chilli and cook for a further 2 minutes.

Stir in the tomatoes and wine and gently simmer for 5 minutes. Add the capsicum, peas and spinach and simmer for 3–4 minutes.

Place the fish and the prawn cutlets in the pan and gently simmer for a further 3–4 minutes or until the fish and prawns are just cooked.

Stir through the cooked rice and season to taste with salt and pepper. Once hot, it is ready to serve.

Waka Nathan was an Auckland (1957–67) and All Blacks (1962–67) player who was never on the losing side in a Test match. He was involved with the New Zealand Maori team as a player (1962–67), selector (1971–77) and manager (1982) and in 2010 became the NZRU's Rugby Legacy Ambassador for RWC 2011.

SERVES 4

CONRAD SMITH'S

Roasted Snapper with Israeli Couscous

This recipe comes from Al Brown's *Go Fish*.

FOR THE MARINADE

½ cup chopped fresh parsley and
   coriander
2 cloves garlic, crushed
1 small red chilli, deseeded and
   finely chopped
1 teaspoon smoked paprika
zest of 2 lemons
¼ cup lemon juice
¼ cup olive oil
1 x 2–3 kilogram whole snapper,
   scaled and gutted

FOR THE ISRAELI COUSCOUS

50 grams butter
1 small onion, finely diced
2 cloves garlic, crushed
zest and juice of 1 lemon
½ cup currants
good pinch of saffron threads,
   soaked in 1 tablespoon warm
   water
1 teaspoon smoked paprika
250 grams Israeli couscous
2½ cups hot chicken stock
knob of butter
¼ cup chopped fresh parsley

Place all the marinade ingredients, except the fish, in a food processor and process to a rough purée.

Make 3 slashes, through to the bone, on each side of the snapper. Place in a large, oiled roasting dish. Brush over most of the marinade, brushing well into the scored flesh on both sides as well as in the gut cavity. Cover and place in the refrigerator to marinate for at least 2 hours. Keep any remaining marinade for cooking the snapper.

Place a large saucepan over a medium-low heat and add the butter, onion, garlic, lemon zest and currants. Cook for 10 minutes, stirring occasionally, until the onion is soft and golden. Add the saffron with its liquid, and the lemon juice and paprika. Cook for a further 5 minutes. Add the couscous, stir, then add the hot stock. Cover with the saucepan lid and cook for 8–10 minutes. Stir through the knob of butter and the chopped parsley. Keep warm or cool then refrigerate and carefully reheat for serving.

Preheat the oven to 180°C.

Remove the snapper from the refrigerator and cover the roasting dish with tinfoil. Cook in the preheated oven for 30 minutes. Remove the snapper from the oven and set the oven to grill. Remove the tinfoil, brush the snapper with the remaining marinade and place under the hot grill to caramelise the presentation side of the snapper. Remove from the grill and set aside to rest for 5 minutes.

Place the whole snapper on a large serving platter with the Israeli couscous to one side.

Conrad Smith made his All Blacks debut at centre in 2004 and has played in over 50 Tests. He has played for Wellington since 2003 and the Hurricanes since 2004 and he captained the Hurricanes in 2012.

SIR WILSON WHINERAY'S
Fish Stew

1 tablespoon olive oil
1 onion, finely chopped
1 stick celery, sliced
1 fennel bulb, very finely sliced
3 cloves garlic, crushed
1 teaspoon curry powder or
   ½ teaspoon red curry paste
1 teaspoon smoked paprika
1 litre fish or chicken stock
2 x 400 gram cans chopped tomatoes
   in juice
2 bay leaves
1 teaspoon sugar
¼ cup cooked orzo or rice
500–600 grams firm white fish
   fillets, cut into chunks
1 kilogram clams, scrubbed
1 tablespoon lemon juice
3 tablespoons roughly chopped
   Italian parsley
salt and freshly ground black pepper
lemon wedges to serve

Heat the oil in a large saucepan over a medium-low heat and cook the onion, celery and fennel until soft but not coloured, about 10 minutes. Stir in the garlic, curry powder or paste and smoked paprika and cook for a further minute. Add the stock, tomatoes, bay leaves and sugar. Bring to the boil, then lower the heat and simmer uncovered for 25 minutes. (You can cool the fish stew base at this stage and freeze until required.)

Add the cooked orzo or rice and the fish and seafood to the pan and gently submerge it in the liquid. Cover and simmer for 4–5 minutes until the fish is just cooked and the clams are open. Gently stir in the lemon juice and parsley and season with salt and pepper to taste.

Serve with lemon wedges and plenty of bread to mop up the juices.

We make this recipe at the beach so use whatever seafood we catch at the time.

Sir Wilson Whineray was an All Blacks prop (1957–65) who captained the side in 30 Tests. He played for Wairarapa (1953), Mid-Canterbury (1954), Manawatu (1955), Canterbury (1955–56), Waikato (1958) and Auckland (1959–66) and is the patron of the New Zealand Rugby Foundation and the NZRU.

Chilli Prawns and Kingfish Sashimi Samoan Style

SERVES 4

CHILLI PRAWNS

12 bamboo skewers

12 large Australian king prawns

1 red chilli, deseeded and finely
   chopped

2 cloves garlic, finely chopped

½ x 165 ml can coconut milk

¼ teaspoon salt

oil for cooking

juice of 1 lime

lime wedges to serve

KINGFISH SASHIMI SAMOAN STYLE

500 grams kingfish, sashimi-grade

1 red chilli, deseeded and finely
   chopped

2 spring onions, very finely sliced

zest and juice of 1 lime

½ x 165 ml can coconut milk

OKA (SAMOAN RAW FISH)
— RECIPE ONLY

500 grams white fish fillets, cut into
   small dice (Rodney likes to use
   kingfish, hapuka or tarakihi)

1 x 165 ml can coconut milk

½ teaspoon salt

1 small red chilli, deseeded and
   finely chopped

2 spring onions, very finely sliced

juice of 2–3 lemons or limes, or
   more to taste

Soak the bamboo skewers in cold water while the prawns are marinating. Remove the body shells and gut tracts of the prawns, but not the heads and tails. Place in a shallow dish.

In a bowl, mix together the chilli, garlic, coconut milk and salt. Pour over the prawns, cover with plastic wrap and place in the refrigerator to marinate for 2 hours.

Preheat the barbecue grill to high and lightly oil.

Remove the marinated prawns from the refrigerator and thread the prawns on to the skewers lengthways, one prawn per skewer. Squeeze over the lime juice.

Grill the prawns for about 40 seconds on each side.

Serve with the lime wedges.

Slice the kingfish into thin slices and place on a platter. Sprinkle over the chilli, spring onions, zest and juice of 1 lime.

Pour the coconut milk into a small bowl and place beside the kingfish slices.

Using chopsticks, pick up a slice of fish and dip into the coconut milk — enjoy.

FOR THE OKA

Place the diced fish in a glass or ceramic bowl. Add the coconut milk, salt, chilli and spring onions. Cover and place in the refrigerator to marinate for 3–4 hours.

Remove from the refrigerator and add the freshly squeezed lemon or lime juice. Mix well to combine and place in a clean glass bowl for serving.

Rodney So'oialo was an All Blacks (2002–09) loose forward and captain (in five Tests). He played for New Zealand Under 21 and New Zealand Sevens, winning a Commonwealth Games gold medal in 2002, as well as Wellington (2000–10) and the Hurricanes (2001–11). He joined the Honda club in Japan in 2011.

DAVID KIRK'S

Rabbit Stew

SERVES 4

David Kirk likes to shoot wild rabbit (it helps landowners out), but to make it easier the rabbits in this recipe were bought from the local butcher.

2 small rabbits
2 tablespoons oil
50 grams butter
1 onion, sliced
1 leek, trimmed and sliced
2 carrots, peeled and cut into chunks
2 sticks celery, thickly sliced
3 cloves garlic, crushed
bouquet garni of 2 bay leaves,
    parsley stalks, sprigs of thyme and
    sweet marjoram
1 tablespoon flour
2 cups hot chicken stock
1 teaspoon dried tarragon (optional)
salt and freshly ground black pepper

Preheat the oven to 180°C. Joint the rabbits by following the bone structure to remove the back legs and the forelegs. Cut the saddle into 2–3 pieces. If you wish, do this ahead of time and use the ribcage and flap of the belly skin to make stock.

Heat the oil in a large frying pan and drop in half the butter. Brown the rabbit in batches over a medium heat, transferring the back legs and saddle pieces to a casserole dish as you go. Place the forelegs on a plate and set aside. You will add these later, as the back legs take longer to cook.

Add the onion and leek and cook until soft, about 10 minutes. Add the carrots, celery and garlic and cook for a further 5 minutes. Place on top of the browned rabbit with the bouquet garni.

Place the remaining butter in the pan and melt, then mix in the flour and stir, scraping the bottom of the pan until the flour is golden. Pour in the hot stock and tarragon, if using, stirring well to loosen any crusty bits. Season with salt and pepper. Pour the sauce over the rabbit and vegetables and cover with baking paper and the casserole lid.

Cook in the preheated oven for 45 minutes. Remove from the oven, add the forelegs and cook for a further 40 minutes or until tender. Serve with a baguette, to mop up all the juices, or mashed potato.

David Kirk played 34 matches at halfback for the All Blacks (1983–87) including 17 Tests and was captain of the Rugby World Cup 1987 winning side. He played for Otago (1982–84) and Auckland (1985–86) and coached Wellington (1993–94). He was inducted into the IRB Hall of Fame in 2011.

SERVES 4

JARRAD HOEATA'S
Thai Green Curry

1 tablespoon vegetable oil
3 tablespoons green curry paste
½ cup chicken stock
1 cup coconut milk
3 kaffir lime leaves
500 grams chicken breast, skinned,
   cut into chunks
150 grams green beans, trimmed
200 grams broccolini or broccoli,
   cut into even lengths
1 tablespoon sugar
2 tablespoons fish sauce
1 tablespoon lime juice
handful of fresh basil leaves

Heat a large deep-sided frying pan over a high heat, add the oil and curry paste and cook for 1 minute until fragrant. Reduce the heat to medium and add the stock, coconut milk and kaffir lime leaves. Cook for 5 minutes. Add the chicken and cook for a further 5 minutes. Add the beans, broccolini or broccoli, sugar, fish sauce and lime juice, and cook for 5 minutes.

Place in a serving bowl, scatter over the basil leaves and serve with steamed rice.

Jarrad Hoeata made his All Blacks debut at lock in 2011 after also representing New Zealand Maori and New Zealand Sevens. He has played provincial rugby for Canterbury and Taranaki and Super Rugby for the Chiefs (2010) and Highlanders (since 2011).

SERVES 4

MARC ELLIS'
Barbecue Chicken

1.5 kilogram whole fresh chicken

¼ cup store-bought dry barbecue rub or dry spice rub of your choice

1 can beer

¼ cup apple juice, preferably poured into a small spray bottle

2 pieces of fruit wood or manuka (tea tree), soaked in cold water overnight or left out in the rain

Preheat the barbecue, getting the charcoal really hot. You will need a kettle barbecue or charcoal barbecue with a hood.

Pat the chicken dry with a paper towel. Rub the barbecue or spice rub evenly over the chicken. Pour half the can of beer into a glass. Insert the half-full beer can into the cavity of the chicken. The legs and beer can should form a reasonably stable tripod so that the chicken will stand upright. Stand the chicken with its beer can upright in a roasting dish and pour in enough water to cover the base of the roasting dish. Spray the chicken with apple juice — this helps to keep the chicken moist during cooking.

Place the soaked wood on top of the very hot coals and replace the rack. Carefully place the roasting dish with the chicken on the rack. Lower the hood and open the vents. Cook for 1¼–1½ hours until the skin is crisp and brown. The drumsticks should move easily when the chicken is cooked. Remove the chicken, can included, from the barbecue and place on a carving board. Leave the chicken to rest for 5 minutes before carefully removing the beer can, which will be very hot. The meat should just about fall off the bone as you carve it.

Tip: The best thing about this recipe is the fun you can have using all kinds of beers. The beer bastes the chicken from the inside and different beers give different flavours — so feel free to experiment.

Marc Ellis played for the All Blacks (1992–95), and holds the record for most All Blacks tries in a Test. He also played for New Zealand Colts (1991), New Zealand Universities (1991–94), Otago (1991–95), North Harbour (1998–2000), the Blues (1999) and the Highlanders (2000).

SERVES 4

AARON SMITH'S
Honey-mustard Chicken

2 tablespoons vegetable oil
25 grams butter
8 chicken drumsticks
4 teaspoons Dijon mustard
2 teaspoons honey

Preheat the oven to 190ºC. Line a shallow baking dish with baking paper. (This helps with the washing up!)

Place the oil and the butter in the baking dish and place in the preheated oven to heat the oil and melt the butter. Remove from the oven and place the drumsticks in the dish, then turn them over, keeping them side by side.

Mix together the Dijon mustard and honey and brush half the mixture over the drumsticks. Turn the drumsticks over again and brush with the remaining mixture.

Cook in the preheated oven for 35–40 minutes, basting with the juices after 20 minutes.

Serve hot with cooked rice and light brown gravy — I add boiling water to a sachet of light gravy mix. Accompany with freshly cut coleslaw.

Aaron Smith made his All Blacks debut at halfback in 2012. He also played for New Zealand Maori in the Centenary Series in 2010 and plays for Manawatu (since 2008) and the Highlanders (since 2011).

BUCK SHELFORD'S
Titi with Watercress and Kumara

From Anne Thorpe's *Kai Ora* television series and book.

SERVES 3–4

2 titi (muttonbirds)
1 large saucepanful of watercress
6 small freshly dug kumara, scrubbed
salt and freshly ground black pepper

Place the titi in a large saucepan, cover with water and bring to the boil. Simmer for 2 hours in a (well-ventilated!) kitchen. Remove the pan from the heat and lift out the titi and set aside. Pour off some of the stock (this removes some of the excess fat) and replace this with the same amount of fresh hot water. Place the watercress and kumara in the liquid and simmer until the kumara are tender, about 15 minutes. This will largely depend on the size of the kumara.

Preheat the grill to hot. Place the titi in a shallow roasting dish and place under the preheated grill for about 10 minutes or until the skin is crisp.

To serve, place the watercress on a serving plate and scatter the kumara around. Break up the titi and place on top of the watercress. Season with salt and pepper.

Buck Shelford was an All Blacks number 8 (1985–90) and captain (in 14 Tests) who was also part of New Zealand Maori (1985–91) and New Zealand Combined Services (1979–85) teams. He played his provincial rugby for Auckland (1982–84) and then North Harbour (1985–91).

05

Beef, Pork and Lamb

VICTOR VITO'S

Beef Wellington

SERVES 2

Recipe based on UK chef Gordon Ramsay's method of preparing and cooking Beef Wellington.

olive oil for cooking

400 gram piece eye fillet

salt and pepper

1–2 teaspoons prepared English mustard

400 grams flat mushrooms, finely chopped

1 tablespoon chopped fresh parsley

4 slices prosciutto or Serrano ham

200 grams frozen puff pastry, thawed

2 egg yolks, lightly beaten with a pinch of salt

flaky sea salt

store-bought beef jus and English mustard to serve

Heat a dash of oil in a frying pan over a high heat and brown the beef on all sides. Season with salt and pepper and set aside on a plate to cool. Spread over the English mustard.

Wipe the frying pan with a paper towel. Place the finely chopped mushrooms in the dry, hot pan and cook until all the water from the mushrooms has evaporated. Stir through the chopped parsley, season with pepper and set aside to cool.

Place a piece of plastic wrap on the benchtop and lay the 4 slices of prosciutto on top, each slice slightly overlapping the last. Spread the mushroom mixture evenly over the prosciutto. Place the beef fillet in the middle, then, using the plastic wrap, roll up into a tight barrel shape. Refrigerate for 15 minutes.

Preheat the oven to 200°C.

On a lightly floured benchtop, roll out the pastry large enough to fit around the meat. Brush the egg wash over the edges, remove the plastic wrap from the beef and place the beef in the middle of the pastry. Fold the pastry over, cutting any excess from the ends, to completely enclose the beef, and turn over.

Place the beef Wellington seam side down in a shallow roasting dish and brush the pastry well with the egg wash. Score the top of the pastry if you wish with a small sharp knife. Place in the refrigerator to chill for 5 minutes. Remove from the refrigerator, brush with egg wash again and sprinkle with a little flaky sea salt.

Cook in the preheated oven for 30 minutes. Remove from the oven and rest for 10 minutes before slicing.

Serve with steamed vegetables and beef jus and English mustard.

Victor Vito debuted as an All Blacks loose forward in 2010 and his representative career includes appearances for New Zealand Schools, Under 19, Under 21 and Sevens. He has played for Wellington since 2006 and for the Hurricanes since 2009.

SERVES 4

ANDREW HORE'S
Venison with Beer and Port

1 tablespoon olive oil

500 grams casserole-cut venison, cut into 2.5 cm dice

2 tablespoons seasoned flour

3–4 rashers bacon, diced (I use wild boar bacon from home)

1 onion, chopped

500 grams pumpkin, peeled and cut into 3 cm pieces

1 carrot, peeled and sliced into rings

¾ cup port or red wine

1 x 400 gram can chopped tomatoes in juice

1 stubbie of beer (I recommend Speight's, as any good Otago man would)

1 teaspoon Vegemite or Marmite

salt and pepper

bouquet garni of 1 bay leaf and 1 sprig each of rosemary and parsley

Preheat the oven to 160°C. Heat the oil in a large frying pan over a medium-high heat. Roll the diced venison in the seasoned flour and brown on all sides. Do this in batches so as not to overcrowd the pan. Transfer the browned venison to an ovenproof casserole dish as you go.

Lower the heat and add the bacon and onion. Cook for 5 minutes until the onion is soft. Add the pumpkin and carrot slices. Pour in the port or red wine and allow to bubble up and reduce slightly. Add the tomatoes, beer and Vegemite or Marmite and stir well, scraping the bottom of the pan. Season to taste with salt and pepper and add to the casserole dish with the bouquet garni. Place in the preheated oven and cook for 3 hours, until the meat is tender and almost falling apart, and the sauce has thickened.

Serve with mashed potatoes — to which I recommend adding a generous knob of butter and a whole egg as well as salt and pepper, as this makes it really rich. Finally, serve with another cold Speight's — this time, for drinking.

Andrew Hore is an experienced hooker with close to 300 first class games to his credit. He made his All Blacks debut in 2002, his provincial rugby debut in 1998 (for Otago) and his Super Rugby debut in 2001 (for the Crusaders). He plays for the Highlanders and Taranaki.

JAMIE MACKINTOSH'S
Venison with Mustard Coating

SERVES 3–4

¼ cup wholegrain mustard

400 grams venison medallions or venison backstrap

1–1½ cups white breadcrumbs, made from stale white bread

½ cup olive oil

beef and red wine jus, store-bought

Rub the mustard evenly over the venison then roll in the breadcrumbs. Place on a plate, cover and refrigerate for about 2 hours. Remove the venison from the refrigerator 10 minutes before cooking.

Pour the olive oil into a large frying pan — it should cover the base — and place on a high heat. Place the coated venison in the pan and cook for 2–3 minutes on each side. Remove from the pan and leave to rest for 3 minutes.

Slice, spoon over a little beef and red wine jus and serve with a kumara or potato mash and steamed asparagus drizzled with lemon juice and black pepper, if desired.

Jamie Mackintosh has a lot of experience in black: he has appeared at prop for New Zealand Secondary Schools (2001–03), Under 19 (2003–04), Under 21 (2005–06), the All Blacks (2008) and the Junior All Blacks (2009). He has played for Southland since 2004 and the Highlanders since 2007.

SERVES 4

ADAM THOMSON'S

Beef Fajitas and Smashed Guacamole

FOR THE FAJITAS

550–600 grams beef eye fillet, cut into finger-long thin strips

1 teaspoon cumin seeds, lightly crushed

½ teaspoon coriander seeds, lightly crushed

½ teaspoon smoked paprika

salt and freshly ground black pepper

2 tablespoons olive oil

2 red onions, peeled with root left intact and cut into wedges

2 yellow capsicums, deseeded and cut into strips

1 red capsicum, deseeded and cut into strips

2 cloves garlic, crushed

1 red chilli, deseeded and finely sliced

1 tablespoon fresh lime juice

2 tablespoons chopped fresh coriander

8 fresh tortillas, warmed

FOR THE GUACAMOLE

2 ripe avocados, cut in half and stone removed

1 small red onion, finely chopped

1 clove garlic, crushed

1 small red chilli, deseeded and finely chopped

1–2 tablespoons fresh lime juice, plus extra to taste

1 ripe tomato, chopped

1 tablespoon chopped fresh coriander

salt

Place the beef in a plastic bag with the cumin and coriander seeds and paprika. Shake it around until the beef strips are well coated in the spice mixture, then set aside while you make the guacamole.

Scoop the flesh from each avocado and place in a bowl. Roughly mash the avocado using a fork. Add the remaining ingredients and mix to combine. Season with salt and extra lime juice to taste. Place the guacamole in a serving bowl and cover well with plastic wrap.

Heat 1 tablespoon of oil in a large frying pan over a medium-high heat. Add the beef strips in batches, so not to overcrowd the pan, and cook for 1–2 minutes, turning once. Transfer cooked beef to a plate and keep warm. Add the remaining tablespoon of oil to the pan and add the onion and capsicum strips. As the capsicums begin to soften, about 2 minutes, add the garlic and chilli and cook for a further minute. Place the cooked beef strips in the pan, add the lime juice and coriander and stir well to combine. Place the fajita mixture into a serving dish.

It is always nice to let people assemble their own fajitas, so have the tortillas heated and ready to go and place the fajita filling and guacamole on the table for everyone to serve themselves.

Adam Thomson debuted as a loose forward for the All Blacks in 2008 and has also played for New Zealand Secondary Schools (2000), Under 19 (2001), Under 21 (2003) and Sevens (2007). He made his provincial rugby debut for Otago in 2004 and his Super Rugby debut in 2006 for the Highlanders.

SERVES 4

KEVEN MEALAMU'S
Teriyaki Beef

½ cup mirin

⅓ cup light soy sauce

1 tablespoon saké

1 teaspoon sesame oil

¼ cup well-packed brown sugar

1½ tablespoons grated fresh ginger

2 cloves garlic, crushed

1 tablespoon sesame seeds

600–700 grams eye fillet, thinly
   sliced

1 x 410 gram can baby corn, cut
   in half, or 2 yellow capsicums,
   deseeded and cut into strips

oil for cooking

2 spring onions, thinly sliced
   (optional)

finely shredded fresh ginger, cooked
   until crisp in a dash of sesame oil
   (optional)

Preheat the grill plate on your barbecue to very hot.

In a large bowl, combine the mirin, soy sauce, saké, sesame oil, brown sugar, ginger, garlic and sesame seeds. Stir in the sliced beef and corn or capsicum, cover and leave to marinate for 10 minutes. Drain the beef mixture, reserving the marinade in a small saucepan.

Lightly oil the heated grill plate (I just use the wok when I'm feeling lazy!) and quickly grill the beef and corn or capsicum in batches. Simmer the marinade over a medium-low heat, uncovered, for 5 minutes. Serve the beef and corn or capsicum drizzled with the hot marinade and sprinkle over the sliced spring onion and crisp shredded ginger if using.

We serve this with noodles or steamed rice. Sometimes we use chicken breast to replace the beef.

Keven Mealamu plays at hooker for the All Blacks (since 2002), the Blues (since 2002) and Auckland (since 1999). He made his Super Rugby debut for the Chiefs in 2000 and is New Zealand's most-capped Super Rugby player.

SERVES 3–4

JERRY COLLINS'
Jambalaya

2 tablespoons vegetable oil

250 grams Spanish or Italian sausages, cut into even-sized pieces

250 grams lean lamb, cut into 2.5 cm pieces

250 grams lean beef, cut into 2.5 cm pieces

1 small red onion, diced

1 stick celery, diced

1 carrot, peeled and diced

1 small red capsicum, deseeded and diced

1 small green capsicum, deseeded and diced

2 cloves garlic, crushed

1 teaspoon Cajun spice seasoning

1 cup long-grain white rice, washed

salt and freshly ground black pepper

zest of 1 lemon or lime

1 tablespoon fresh thyme leaves

6 basil leaves, torn into pieces

1 cup hot beef stock

½ cup hot water

Heat 1 tablespoon of the oil in a large, lidded, deep-sided frying pan over a medium-high heat and brown the meat on all sides in batches. Set aside on a plate.

Lower the heat slightly and add the remaining oil. Then add the diced onion, celery, carrot and capsicum and cook for 5 minutes or until they are just beginning to colour. Add the garlic and Cajun spice seasoning and cook for 1 minute. Add the rice, season with salt and pepper and cook for a further minute. Return the browned meat to the frying pan with the lemon or lime zest, herbs, beef stock and water. Bring to the boil, cover with the lid, lower the heat and simmer for 20 minutes until the rice is cooked. (If you don't have a frying pan with a lid, transfer to a saucepan before returning the meat.)

Serve in a large bowl.

Jerry Collins was an All Blacks loose forward (2001–07) and captain in three Tests. He was also part of New Zealand Schools and Colts teams and played for Wellington (1999–07) and the Hurricanes (2001–07) before joining northern hemisphere teams including Toulon and Ospreys.

MAKES 4

Bagel Burgers

FOR THE MINCE PATTIES

400 grams premium beef mince

2 spring onions, trimmed and finely
  chopped

2 cloves garlic, crushed

1 teaspoon beef stock powder

1 teaspoon light soy sauce

2 eggs, lightly beaten

½ teaspoon freshly ground black
  pepper

1 ripe tomato, halved, core removed
  and finely chopped

oil for cooking

FOR THE BURGERS

4 plain or sesame seed bagels, cut in
  half and toasted

8 tablespoons mayonnaise

4 tablespoons of your favourite
  tomato sauce

4 lettuce leaves, washed and dried

4 slices of cheese

1 red onion, thinly sliced

1 avocado, halved and stone
  removed

Place all the ingredients for the patties, except the tomato, into a large bowl and mix well to combine. Stir through the chopped tomato. Divide the meat mixture into 4 and form into patties.

Heat a dash of oil in a large non-stick frying pan over a medium heat. Place the patties in the pan, pushing down on them as they cook to flatten. Cook for 8–10 minutes, turning once until the patties feel firm to the touch. Transfer to a plate ready to assemble into burgers.

Spread the bottom of each toasted bagel with 1 tablespoon of mayonnaise and some sauce.

Layer each bagel with a lettuce leaf, a cooked meat pattie, a slice of cheese, some red onion and avocado.

Spread the remaining mayonnaise on each of the bagel tops and place on the burger stacks.

Frae Wilson played all five Junior World Championship matches at halfback for New Zealand Under 20 in 2009, the same year he made his debut for Wellington. He made his Super Rugby debut for the Hurricanes in 2012.

SERVES 6–8

RICHIE McCAW'S
Topside Supreme

oil for cooking
1.5 kilogram topside beef
1 onion, chopped
2 cups water
2 tablespoons white wine vinegar
1 tablespoon Worcestershire sauce
2 teaspoons beef stock powder
bouquet garni of 1 bay leaf, 2 sprigs
   of thyme and a few parsley stalks
   or ½ teaspoon dried mixed herbs
soft butter and flour for thickening
   juices

Place a dash of oil in a large saucepan over a high heat and brown the piece of meat on all sides. Set aside on a plate.

Lower the heat, add the onion and cook until lightly golden, about 10 minutes.

Return the meat to the saucepan, add onion, water, vinegar, Worcestershire sauce, beef stock powder and bouquet garni and cover with the saucepan lid. Cook on a very low simmer for 5–6 hours until the meat is tender and falling apart. You can also cook this in the oven at 150°C, or in a slow cooker.

Remove the meat from the saucepan and keep warm. You should be able to pull the meat apart with 2 forks to serve.

Thicken the juices with a paste made from equal quantities of soft butter and flour. Whisk into the juices.

Serve with plenty of mashed potato, vegetables and the meat sauce.

Richie McCaw made his All Blacks debut in 2001, holds the records for most Test appearances and most appearances and wins as captain, and lead the team to victory at RWC 2011. He has played for Canterbury since 2000 and for the Crusaders since 2001, winning numerous Super Rugby titles.

SERVES 4

MELODIE ROBINSON'S

Pork Belly with Baby Beetroot and Lentils

FOR THE PORK

1–1.2 kilogram pork belly, skin well-scored

1 tablespoon olive oil

1 tablespoon flaky sea salt

FOR THE BEETROOT

400 grams baby beetroot, peeled and trimmed

2 cups water

½ cup malt vinegar

½ cup brown sugar

FOR THE LENTILS

1 tablespoon olive oil

1 clove garlic, thinly sliced

2 x 400 gram cans lentils, drained and rinsed

1 tablespoon red wine vinegar

½ cup chicken stock

2 teaspoons fresh thyme leaves

Preheat the oven to 180°C. Rub the pork belly with the oil and then the salt, rubbing the salt in well where the skin is scored. Place skin side down in a roasting dish, cover, and roast for 1 hour. Uncover and turn the pork belly over to roast for a further hour until the skin is golden and crisp. If the skin is not crisp, turn the oven to the grill setting and grill for about 10 minutes, watching so it does not burn. Leave to rest in a warm oven for 10 minutes before slicing.

Place the beetroot in a saucepan with the water, vinegar and sugar. Bring to the boil, lower the heat, cover and simmer for 30 minutes until the beetroot is tender and the liquid a little syrupy.

Heat the olive oil in another small saucepan, add the sliced garlic and cook gently for 1 minute, making sure the garlic does not burn and take on a bitter flavour. Add the lentils, vinegar, stock and thyme leaves and cook for 5 minutes or until heated through. Season to taste.

Slice the pork and serve with the beetroot and lentils.

Melodie Robinson was a loose forward who played for Wellington (1996–99), Auckland (2001–02) and the Black Ferns (1996–02), including two Women's Rugby World Cups. She was the first woman to commentate an international rugby match and is a presenter and commentator for Sky Sport and Prime.

SERVES 4–6

COREY FLYNN'S
Spare Ribs

1 kilogram pork spare ribs, cut into pieces

FOR THE MARINADE
¼ cup hoisin sauce
¼ cup oyster sauce
2 tablespoons light soy sauce
2 teaspoons sesame oil
½ teaspoon Chinese five-spice powder

Place the spare ribs in a glass or ceramic dish.

Combine the marinade ingredients and pour over the ribs, tossing to coat evenly. Cover and refrigerate for 1 hour.

Preheat the grill. Line a baking tray with 2 layers of foil and place a grill rack on top of the baking tray.

Arrange the marinated ribs on the grill rack and place under the grill for 10 minutes, turning occasionally. Keep the leftover marinade to brush on while cooking. Remove the ribs from the grill, brush with any extra marinade and return to the grill for a further 10 minutes.

Alternatively, the ribs can be placed in a lightly floured oven bag (read the cooking instructions on the oven bag packet) and cooked in the oven at 180°C for about 30 minutes or until the ribs are tender. Remove from the oven bag. You may also wish to brown them quickly under a hot grill for extra colour and stickiness.

Serve the spare ribs with a sweet chilli sauce or, as the boys like them, just as they are!

Corey Flynn has appeared at prop for New Zealand Under 16 (1997), Secondary Schools (1998), Under 19 (2000), Colts (2001–02), New Zealand Maori in 2002–05 and 2010, the Junior All Blacks (2005–07) and made his All Blacks debut in 2003. He plays for Canterbury and the Crusaders.

SERVES 8

JIMMY COWAN'S
Roast Pork

1.5–2 kilogram roast of pork on the
  bone, skin well scored
2 tablespoons olive oil
1 tablespoon flaky sea salt
4 apples — Braeburn work well

Preheat the oven to 200°C. Place the pork in a roasting dish and rub the skin with the oil, then the salt.

Roast in the preheated oven for 30 minutes then lower the temperature to 180°C and roast for 1½ hours. Cut the apples in half and place around the pork, one hour before the end of cooking. At the end of the cooking time, pierce the thickest part of the roast with a fine skewer — the juices should run clear.

Remove from the oven and rest in a warm place for 15 minutes.

Carve off the crackling in a single piece and portion it before carving the meat.

Serve pork with the crackling and apples along with roasted root vegetables and peas or green beans.

Jimmy Cowan made his All Blacks debut at halfback in 2004. He has played for Southland since 2000 and for the Highlanders since 2003. He brought up 100 appearances for the Highlanders in 2012.

BEN FRANKS'

Easy Apricot and Mustard Pork Chops

SERVES 4

4 pork chops
2 tablespoons apricot jam
2 tablespoons Dijon mustard
1 shallot, finely chopped

Preheat the grill to high. Place the pork chops on a grilling rack and grill for 6 minutes, turning once.

In a small bowl, mix together the apricot jam and Dijon mustard. Brush half on one side of the grilled pork chops and return to the grill for a further 2 minutes. Turn the pork chops over, brush with the remaining mixture and top with the shallot. Grill for 1 minute.

Serve the grilled pork chops with steamed greens and orange kumara mash.

Ben Franks made his debut as an All Blacks prop in 2008 against Munster. He has previously appeared in New Zealand Under 19 (2003) and Under 21 (2005) sides, made his provincial rugby debut for Canterbury in 2005 and his Super Rugby debut in 2006.

SERVES 4
HUNGRY PLAYERS

PIRI WEEPU'S
Boil-up with Fancy Buttermilk Dough Boys

1 kilogram pork bones

4 potatoes, skin on, scrubbed and
   cut into even-sized chunks

4 small red kumara, lightly peeled
   and cut into even-sized chunks

1 cup flour

½ teaspoon salt

1 teaspoon baking powder

1 teaspoon baking soda

15 grams very cold butter, cut into
   small pieces

¼ cup buttermilk

1 large bunch watercress, excess
   stalk removed

Place the pork bones in a large saucepan and cover with cold water. Bring to the boil, cover with the lid and keep boiling for about 45 minutes. Remove from the heat.

Place the potatoes and kumara in a separate saucepan and cook until nearly tender, about 15 minutes. Drain. Add the potatoes and kumara to the pork bones and allow the flavours to mingle.

Place the flour, salt, baking powder and baking soda in a food processor. Add the butter and pulse until the mixture resembles fine breadcrumbs. Add the buttermilk and pulse until the dough forms a ball.

On a lightly floured benchtop, roll the dough out into a sausage shape and cut into short lengths.

Return the boil-up to a low heat, add the watercress and allow to wilt.

Add the dough boys to the saucepan and stir gently as needed to keep them separated. Cook until they just set — any more and they will break up.

Ladle the boil-up into warmed bowls for serving. I like to serve a boil-up with Mum's fried bread as well.

Piri Weepu debuted as an All Blacks halfback in 2004 and has also played for New Zealand Under 21 (2004), New Zealand Maori since 2005 and the Junior All Blacks (2005). He has played Super Rugby for the Hurricanes (2004–11) and the Blues (since 2012) and provincial rugby for Wellington since 2003.

SERVES 8

ISRAEL DAGG'S
Roast Leg of Lamb
Sir Colin Meads also loves to cook roast leg of lamb.

2 kilogram leg of lamb

sprigs of rosemary

5 cloves garlic, peeled and thickly
sliced

salt

6 large floury potatoes, skin on,
scrubbed

olive oil for drizzling

pepper

Preheat the oven to 220°C. Line a roasting dish with baking paper.

Using a small sharp knife, pierce the fat of the leg of lamb and place into each hole a sprig of rosemary and a thick slice of garlic. Sprinkle over a little salt and set aside while preparing the potatoes.

Slice the potatoes about 3 mm thick and lay them in the prepared roasting dish, drizzling over a little olive oil and season with salt and pepper as you layer.

Place the prepared leg of lamb straight onto one of the oven racks and place the roasting dish of potatoes directly underneath (so it will catch all the fat and juices from the roasting lamb) and roast for 20 minutes. Lower the oven temperature to 200°C and roast for a further 40 minutes. This will give you lamb that is pink and juicy.

Remove the lamb from the oven and leave to rest for 10 minutes before carving. (Cover loosely with foil then place a clean tea towel over the top to keep it warm.)

Serve with the crisp layered potatoes, a big bowl of green peas and redcurrant jelly.

Israel Dagg made his All Blacks debut at fullback in 2010 after appearances for New Zealand Schools (2006), Under 19 (2007) and Sevens (2007–08). He has played for Hawke's Bay since 2006 and made his Super Rugby debut in 2009 for the Highlanders.

Sir Colin Meads was an All Blacks lock and loose forward (1957–71), holds the record for most matches for the All Blacks (133) and was named New Zealand's Player of the Century in 1999. He has also been an All Blacks selector and manager and NZRU Councillor, and played for King Country (1955–72).

WYATT CROCKETT'S

Slow-cooked Moroccan Lamb Shanks

SERVES 4

1 tablespoon olive oil

4 large lamb shanks

1 onion, chopped

2 cloves garlic, sliced

1 tablespoon grated fresh ginger

1 teaspoon turmeric

1 teaspoon ground cumin

½ teaspoon cardamom pods

¼ teaspoon crushed chilli flakes

1 tablespoon brown sugar

1 x 400 gram can chopped tomatoes in juice

2 cups chicken or vegetable stock

salt and pepper

1 cup peeled and diced (2 cm) pumpkin

2 potatoes, diced (2 cm)

1 orange kumara, cut into 2 cm dice

¼ cup roughly chopped fresh parsley

Place the oil in a large frying pan over a medium-high heat and brown the lamb shanks on all sides. Place in a slow cooker.

Lower the heat to medium-low, add the onion to the pan and cook for 5 minutes, stirring occasionally. Add the garlic and ginger and cook for a further minute. Add the turmeric, cumin, cardamom pods and chilli flakes. Cook for 2 minutes, stirring continuously. Add the brown sugar, tomatoes and stock and bring to the boil. Add the salt and pepper to taste, and pour into the slow cooker with the lamb shanks.

Add the diced vegetables, cover with the lid and set the slow cooker on low for at least 6 hours or until the lamb is tender and begins to fall off the bone. (I like to cook these the day before, cool and refrigerate overnight so the fat comes to the surface and can be easily removed. Then I gently reheat to serve.)

Stir through the chopped parsley, if using, and serve with couscous.

Wyatt Crockett made his All Blacks propping debut in 2009 following selections in New Zealand Under 19 (2002) and Under 21 (2004) sides. He has played for Canterbury since 2005 and for the Crusaders since 2006, playing in his 100th Super Rugby game in 2012.

ROBBIE FRUEAN'S

Honey-hoisin Grilled Lamb Chops

SERVES 4

8 loin lamb chops, preferably
   3.5–4 cm thick
flaky sea salt

FOR THE MARINADE
3 tablespoons vegetable oil
3 tablespoons light soy sauce
2 tablespoons hoisin sauce
2 tablespoons lemon juice
2 tablespoons Dijon mustard
1 tablespoon sesame oil
1 tablespoon liquid honey
1 onion, very finely chopped
¼ cup chopped fresh Italian parsley
2 tablespoons chopped fresh
   rosemary leaves
freshly ground black pepper

Using a small sharp knife, score across the fat on the side of the lamb chops and rub in a little flaky sea salt. Set aside on a large plate while you make the marinade.

In a medium-sized bowl, mix together the marinade ingredients. (You could mix the ingredients in a jar as the marinade can be kept in the refrigerator for up to 5 days.)

Brush some of the marinade over the meat and marinate for at least 30 minutes.

Preheat the barbecue grill to a medium heat.

Grill the lamb chops with the fat side down until the fat is well browned and crisp. They should sit up nicely for you or you may have to do this in batches and hold them in place with long-handled tongs. Grill the lamb chops for about 5 minutes on each side, turning once. Brush with extra marinade as you grill. Cooking time will depend upon the thickness of the chops but they are delicious if pink and juicy in the centre.

Serve with green vegetables or a simple green salad and crumble over a little feta cheese if you wish. Freshly dug potatoes, cooked in lightly salted water, go down a treat as well.

Robbie Fruean played at centre for New Zealand Under 19, earning the IRB's Under 19 Player of the Year Award in 2007. He made his provincial rugby debut the same year for Wellington and his Super Rugby debut for the Hurricanes (2009). He has played for the Canterbury and the Crusaders since 2010.

06

Desserts and Cakes

SERVES 8

JEROME KAINO'S

Banana Cake

This cake is a version of Jo Seagar's Family Banana Cake from *A Treasury of New Zealand Baking*.

100 grams butter, softened

1 cup caster sugar

3 eggs

3 ripe bananas, mashed

½ cup milk

1 teaspoon baking soda

200 ml natural yoghurt — buffalo
works well

2 cups flour

3 teaspoons baking powder

FOR THE LEMON ICING

50 grams butter, melted

2 tablespoons boiling water

zest and juice of 1 lemon

3½ cups icing sugar

pared rind of 1–2 lemons, cut into
fine shreds (optional)

Preheat the oven to 160°C. Line a 20 cm round tin with baking paper.

Beat the butter and sugar together until light and creamy. Beat in the eggs, one at a time. Add the mashed banana and beat well.

Heat the milk until just below boiling point and stir in the baking soda. Stir into the banana mixture with the yoghurt.

Sift in the flour and baking powder and fold together until just combined. Pour into the prepared tin.

Bake in the preheated oven for 50–55 minutes or until a skewer inserted in the centre of the cake comes out clean. Cool in the tin for 5 minutes before cooling on a wire rack.

To make the lemon icing, melt the butter in a bowl in the microwave, then add the boiling water, lemon zest and juice. Sift in the icing sugar and stir until smooth. Spread over the cooled cake. If you want your icing to drizzle over the cake, add a little extra lemon juice or water.

Blanch the pared lemon shreds, if using, in boiling water for 20 seconds, drain, refresh under cold water, then spread onto paper towels to dry. Scatter over the wet icing.

Jerome Kaino made his All Blacks debut as a loose forward in 2006 and has also appeared for New Zealand Schools (2001), Under 19 (2002), Under 21 (2003–04), New Zealand Sevens (2005) and the Junior All Blacks (2005). He debuted for Auckland in 2004 and for the Blues in 2004.

SERVES 4–6

SIR GRAHAM HENRY'S
Apple Sponge

FOR THE APPLES

6 Granny Smith apples, peeled,
  cored and sliced
1 cup water
½ cup sugar

FOR THE SPONGE

125 grams butter, softened
½ cup sugar
1 egg
1 cup flour
2 teaspoons baking powder
¼–½ cup milk
1 tablespoon icing sugar for dusting

Preheat the oven to 190°C. Lightly grease a 4-cup capacity ovenproof dish. Place the sliced apple in a saucepan with the water and sugar. Cover and cook the apples until soft, about 8 minutes. Place in the ovenproof dish and keep hot.

To prepare the sponge, place the butter and sugar in a bowl and beat until pale and creamy. Add the egg and beat well. Sift the flour and baking powder together and fold into the creamed mixture. Add enough milk to make the batter a soft dropping consistency, using more if necessary.

Spoon the mixture evenly over the hot apples. Bake in the preheated oven for 30 minutes or until the sponge is golden and springs back when lightly touched. Sift over the icing sugar and serve hot with vanilla custard or fresh cream, or both.

Sir Graham Henry was Coach of the All Blacks (2004–11), including their victory at RWC 2011. He has previously coached Auckland (1992–97), the Blues (1996–98), Wales (1998–2002), and the British and Irish Lions (2001). He has won the IRB's Coach of the Year Award three times.

SERVES 10

LACHIE MUNRO'S
Chocolate Brownie

2 cups caster sugar
⅔ cup cocoa
½ cup flour
1 teaspoon baking powder
4 eggs, lightly beaten
1 teaspoon vanilla extract
250 grams butter, melted
1½ cups dark chocolate baking chips
fresh fruit to serve
1 x 200 gram pouch of mascarpone
2 tablespoons honey

Preheat the oven to 160°C. Line a 20 cm square tin with baking paper.

Sift the sugar, cocoa, flour and baking powder into a large bowl and make a well in the centre. Add the eggs, vanilla and melted butter to the well and stir to combine. Fold through the chocolate chips.

Pour into the prepared tin and bake in the preheated oven for 40–45 minutes.

Cut while still warm into small squares and place on a serving platter with slices or whole pieces of seasonal fruit. Place a large dollop of mascarpone on the plate and drizzle with your favourite honey.

Lachie Munro has played at wing, fullback and first five-eighth for Auckland (2006–07), Northland (since 2008) and the Blues, for whom he debuted in 2009. He has also played for New Zealand Sevens and New Zealand Under 21 (2007).

SERVES 8

BEN HURST'S

Lime and White Chocolate Cheesecake

FOR THE BASE
250 grams digestive biscuits
100 grams butter, melted

FOR THE FILLING
750 grams cream cheese
1 cup caster sugar
150 ml cream
150 grams white chocolate
zest and juice of 2–3 limes
4 eggs

RASPBERRY SAUCE
500 grams raspberries
1 cup icing sugar
juice of 1 lemon

TO ASSEMBLE
fresh berries, mint leaves, shaved
    coconut, passionfruit pulp and the
    zest of 2 extra limes to decorate

Preheat the oven to 120°C. Lightly grease the base and sides of a 23 cm springform tin. Place the digestive biscuits in a food processor and process into crumbs. Transfer to a bowl, pour in the melted butter and mix to combine. Press the base mixture into the prepared springform tin, cover with plastic wrap and place in the refrigerator to chill while making the filling.

For the filling, place the cream cheese and sugar in a large bowl and beat until smooth. (An electric beater works well here.) Scrape down the sides occasionally. Place the cream and chocolate in a microwave-proof bowl and microwave on high for 1 minute. Remove from the microwave and stir until the mixture is smooth. Set aside. Mix the lime zest and juice into the cream cheese mixture. Beat the eggs in, one at a time. Lastly, fold through the cream and chocolate mixture.

Remove the base from the refrigerator and pour in the filling, smoothing the top with a spatula. Place the cheesecake in the preheated oven and bake for 1 hour or until the mixture has nearly set. Remove from the oven and cool then cover and refrigerate until firm.

To prepare the sauce, blend the ingredients in a food processor until shiny. Press through a sieve to extract the raspberry seeds.

Remove the cheesecake from the springform tin and place on a serving plate. Decorate the top with fresh berries, mint leaves, shaved coconut, passionfruit pulp and extra lime zest. Serve with the raspberry sauce.

Ben Hurst played over 50 games at halfback for Canterbury (1999–2003) and the Crusaders (2000–03) and captained Canterbury in 2003.

SERVES 6

THE CHIEFS'
Apple Cake

Sometimes when the nutritionist isn't watching, The Chiefs' professional development manager, Judy Clement, likes to whip the boys up a favourite treat. This one is popular.

FOR THE CAKE

1 cup self-raising flour

1 teaspoon baking powder

2 teaspoons ground cinnamon

¾ cup caster sugar

⅓ cup milk

50 grams butter, melted

2 eggs, lightly beaten

4 medium-sized apples, peeled, cored and chopped (we used Braeburn)

FOR THE GLAZE

75 grams butter, softened

½ cup caster sugar

1 teaspoon vanilla extract or paste

1 egg

icing sugar for dusting

Preheat the oven to 160°C on fan bake. Line a 20 cm round cake tin with baking paper.

In a mixing bowl, sift together the flour, baking powder and cinnamon. Stir in the sugar and make a well in the centre. Pour in the milk, butter and eggs and gently mix with a wooden spoon until combined. Mix in the chopped apples.

Pour the cake mixture into the prepared tin and bake in the preheated oven for 40 minutes.

For the glaze, place the butter and sugar in a small bowl and beat until light and creamy. Add the vanilla and egg and continue beating until well combined. Spoon the glaze over the cake and return to the oven for a further 20–25 minutes or until a skewer inserted in the centre of the cake comes out clean.

Remove cake from the oven and allow to cool in the tin for 20 minutes. Dust with icing sugar and serve warm with custard — delicious.

SERVES 8

CHARLIE FAUMUINA'S
Chocolate Cake

FOR THE CAKE

3 cups flour

3 teaspoons baking powder

3 tablespoons cocoa

1¾ cups caster sugar

200 grams butter

1½ cups water

2 teaspoons vinegar

2 teaspoons vanilla extract or vanilla
paste

200 grams dark chocolate, broken
into small pieces

½ cup cream

1½ cups milk

½ teaspoon baking soda

3 eggs, lightly beaten

FOR THE ICING

4 cups icing sugar

3 tablespoons cocoa

fresh or caramelised walnuts to
decorate (optional)

Preheat the oven to 180°C. Line a 22 cm or 23 cm round cake tin with baking paper.

In a large mixing bowl, sift together the flour, baking powder and cocoa. Stir in the sugar and make a well in the centre. Place the butter, water, vinegar and vanilla in a small saucepan and heat until the butter has melted.

Place the chocolate and cream in a microwave-proof bowl and microwave on high for 1 minute. Remove and stir gently until combined. Bring the milk to boiling point in a small saucepan and stir in the baking soda.

Pour the butter, chocolate and milk mixtures, along with the eggs, into the dry ingredients and whisk gently until just combined. Pour the cake batter into the prepared tin.

Place in the preheated oven for 35–40 minutes or until a skewer inserted in the centre of the cake comes out clean. Remove the cake from the oven and allow to cool before removing from the tin.

For the icing, sift the sugar and cocoa in to a bowl. Add the butter and mix in with enough water until you have a spreadable consistency.

Ice with chocolate icing once cool and, if you wish, decorate with fresh or caramelised walnuts.

Charlie Faumuina is a prop for the Blues (since 2009) and Auckland (since 2007) and played for New Zealand Under 21 in 2007.

SERVES 4

CHRIS POLLOCK'S
Apple Crumble

2 x 380 gram cans sliced apples or
   6 Braeburn apples, stewed
1 cup flour
1 teaspoon baking powder
1 teaspoon ground cinnamon or
   ½ teaspoon ground cardamom
½ cup soft brown sugar
¼ cup rolled oats
100 grams chilled butter, cut into
   small dice
70 grams slivered almonds
vanilla ice-cream to serve

Preheat the oven to 190°C. Lightly grease a 4-cup capacity ovenproof dish. Place the apples in the prepared dish.

Place the flour, baking powder, cinnamon or cardamom, sugar and rolled oats in a food processor and process for 10 seconds. Add the chilled diced butter and process until the mixture resembles coarse breadcrumbs. Stir through the slivered almonds. Spoon the crumble mixture evenly over the apples and cook in the preheated oven for 20–25 minutes, until golden and bubbling.

Serve with vanilla ice-cream.

Chris Pollock is one of New Zealand's most experienced referees. He made his first class refereeing debut in 2000 and refereed his first Test in 2005 and first Super Rugby match in 2006. He was an assistant referee at RWC 2011 and is a member of the IRB's International Referees Panel.

SERVES 4–6

MRS WHITELOCK'S

Self-saucing Pudding

1 cup flour
2 heaped teaspoons baking powder
½ cup caster sugar
¼ cup cocoa
250 ml milk
90 grams butter, melted
2 eggs, lightly beaten

FOR THE TOPPING
1 cup brown sugar
1½ tablespoons cocoa
250 ml boiling water
crème fraîche and raspberry jam to
   serve

Preheat the oven to 180°C. Lightly grease a 4-cup capacity ovenproof dish.

Sift the flour, baking powder, caster sugar and cocoa into a bowl. Add the milk, butter, eggs and vanilla and beat until combined (an electric beater works well here). Pour into the prepared ovenproof dish.

Mix the brown sugar and cocoa together and sprinkle over the pudding mixture. Pour the boiling water over the back of a large spoon onto the pudding mixture. This helps distribute the topping evenly. Place in the preheated oven and cook for 40–45 minutes.

Spoon into individual dessert bowls and serve with a good dollop of crème fraîche and a teaspoonful of raspberry jam.

The Whitelock Boys Adam, George, Sam and Luke Whitelock all play for Canterbury and the Crusaders. George also played for Otago, New Zealand Under 19 (2005) and Under 21 (2007) and made his All Blacks debut in 2009. Sam made his All Blacks debut in 2010 and Luke captained the Junior World Championship-winning New Zealand Under 20 side in 2011.

MAKES 12

CHRIS LAIDLAW'S

Lemon Shortbread with Roasted Rhubarb

FOR THE SHORTBREAD

100 grams butter, softened but not melted
½ cup rice flour
½ cup cornflour
½ cup icing sugar
½ cup ground almonds
1 tablespoon grated lemon zest

FOR THE RHUBARB

6 stalks rhubarb, cut into even-sized pieces about the size of your thumb
sugar for sprinkling

TO ASSEMBLE

12 tablespoons Greek-style yoghurt
lemon curd for drizzling
extra icing sugar for dusting (optional)

Place all the shortbread ingredients in a mixing bowl and mix well to combine (it will be a little crumbly). Form the mixture into a ball, then shape the dough into a cylinder about 5 cm in diameter. Wrap well in greaseproof paper and place in the refrigerator for 1 hour.

Preheat the oven to 150°C. Line 2 baking trays with baking paper or lightly grease. Cut the chilled dough into thin rounds, about 5 mm thick, and place 6 rounds on each of the prepared baking trays. Bake the shortbread, a tray at a time, for 15–20 minutes or until lightly golden. Keep an eye on them after 15 minutes so they do not colour too much. Remove the shortbread from the oven and leave to cool and crisp on the baking trays before removing and storing in an airtight container.

For the rhubarb, preheat the oven to 180°C. Line a shallow baking tray with baking paper. Place the rhubarb in the prepared tray and sprinkle well with the sugar. Roast the rhubarb in the preheated oven for 10–12 minutes or until tender. Pierce with a skewer to test if it is tender.

To serve, spread 1 tablespoon of yoghurt on to each shortbread biscuit, top with roasted rhubarb and drizzle over a little lemon curd. Finish with icing sugar if you wish.

Chris Laidlaw played at halfback for the All Blacks (1963–68) and captained the team in 1968. He played most of his provincial rugby for Otago (1962–67) and also for Oxford University and Lyon University while studying overseas.

JOHN STURGEON'S

Delicious Steamed Pudding

SERVES 6

2–3 tablespoons golden syrup
100 grams butter
½ cup caster sugar
2 eggs, lightly beaten
1 teaspoon vanilla extract
1 cup self-raising flour
¼ cup milk

Thoroughly grease a 4-cup capacity ceramic bowl. Cut out rounds of baking paper and tinfoil larger than the bowl to make a lid.

Place a large saucepan of water on to boil. There should be enough water in the saucepan to come three-quarters of the way up the pudding bowl. Place an upturned saucer or trivet (if you have one) in the bottom of the saucepan for the bowl to sit on. This prevents the bowl from cracking. Place the golden syrup in the base of the bowl.

Place the butter and sugar in a microwave-proof bowl, microwave until just melted then stir. Add the eggs and vanilla, beating well, then fold in the flour. Fold through the milk to just combine and place in the prepared bowl.

Cover with the paper and tinfoil lid and tie down with string. For ease of removing the bowl once the pudding is cooked, make a handle out of string as well. Place the pudding bowl in the saucepan of boiling water, cover with the saucepan lid and boil for 1¼ hours. If necessary, top up the boiling water during cooking.

Carefully remove the pudding from the saucepan, remove the paper and tinfoil lid and place a serving plate over the top of the bowl. Invert the pudding onto the plate.

Serve with vanilla custard or make a simple sauce by gently melting a little golden syrup with cream and a knob of butter.

John Sturgeon was elected to the NZRU Council in 1987 and has served numerous roles including managing the New Zealand Colts, Northern Maori, New Zealand Sevens and the All Blacks (1988–91) and was elected President (2009–10). He received an MBE in 1991 for his services to sport.

Dawsons gladly offered The Kelliher Estate as a location for one of the photo shoots for this book.
Dawsons also granted the New Zealand Rugby Foundation an opportunity to host an exclusive
fundraising dinner at their magnificent venue.

Set within sub-tropical and native gardens on Puketutu Island in the Manukau Harbour, The Kelliher
Estate is truly an exceptional property suitable for all occasions. Dawsons bring to the table their
immense experience, masterful cuisine and an exceptional talent for making every event one of a kind.

www.dawsons.co.nz

THE KELLIHER ESTATE
PUKETUTU ISLAND

Dawsons
Cuisine · Events · Venues

Index